To Dad, Happy Fathers day.
I love you.

Billy.

BACKPACKING MADE EASY

Michael Abel

Library of Congress Cataloging in Publication Data

Abel, Michael, 1947 –
    Backpacking made easy.

    Bibliography: p.
    Includes index.
    1. Backpacking.   I. Title.
GV199.6.A23   1975   796.5   75-8529

REVISED EDITION

NATUREGRAPH PRESS

ISBN   0-87961-040-9   Paper Edition
ISBN   0-87961-041-7   Cloth Edition

Published by Naturegraph Publishers, Healdsburg, CA   95448

TABLE OF CONTENTS

Page

How glorious a greeting the sun
gives the mountains! To behold
this alone is worth the pains of any
excursion a thousand times over.

John Muir

ACKNOWLEDGMENTS

The photograph on the cover and those throughout the book were taken by the author. Illustrations drawn by Tony Shearer are used where indicated; others were adapted from his original work (by Teddi Heater) for use in this book. Grizzly Bear painted by Douglas Andrews. Black Bear drawn by Donald Malick. Special thanks are extended to Helen Maris for her help in lending technical advice and typing skills.

CHAPTER 1

AN INTRODUCTION TO BACKPACKING

In our modern world of airplanes, autos and automation we seldom have the opportunity to relax and appreciate the beauty of our world. Backpacking presents us with that opportunity. It is one of the few sports which is open to almost everyone, be he young or old. It is also a sport in which everyone can participate, not just spectate. Furthermore, it is a sport in which everyone wins, and the prizes are many.

Contrary to popular conception, backpacking is a very safe sport. Backpackers seldom get hurt. It is a healthful sport. The fresh mountain air invigorates your body, cleanses your skin, clears your lungs, and sharpens your mind. Best of all, it is cheap. In these days of inflation who ever heard of a family of four spending a weekend away from home on a fabulous vacation for twenty dollars?

Such are the pleasures open to one who is willing to expend a little energy and a little money. In return, Mother Nature will give you much and extract nothing but a little of your energy.

Just to give the reader an idea of the rewards available to him, I am compelled to relate a story told me this past summer.

While wending my way up a pass in the Sierra Nevada, I overtook a gentleman in his late fifties. He was taking some snapshots of a canyon. We started a conversation, and he told me this story.

Two years before, at the age of fifty-six, he had visited his doctor. At that time the circulation in his legs was bad and he lost his wind with the slightest exertion. Just going up a flight of stairs required great effort. The doctor, who had been prescribing medication, alluded to the numerous pills the gentleman had been ingesting and said, "Now you can do one of two things. You can take these things and I might be able to keep you alive for the next ten years, or you can get out and get some fresh air and exercise and live to be a hundred."

Well, out he was, and spry as most men half his age. His secret fountain of youth was nothing more than an occasional evening walk at home and a little fresh mountain air every once in a while. The pain in his legs was long gone, and his breathing was normal.

Such are the incalculable health benefits available to those who seek Nature's joys.

I, myself, a city dweller, am a frequent victim of common colds. Yet in all my days in the mountains, I have never had even a sniffle.

This is really not unusual. Mother Nature in her pristine state harbors few malignant germs. These harmful gremlins prefer the city which provides them with a better atmosphere in which to propagate themselves.

In quest of this healthful life, more and more people are taking to the mountains.

In the last ten years, backpacking has undergone a virtual revolution as a sport. Trails that were once trodden by only a handful of people every summer are now packed by legions of summer mountaineers. People of all ages and occupations flock to our wilderness areas to roam the trails for a few days or weeks to enjoy nature's beauty. Business executives leave their desks, chemists leave their labs, and students lay their studies aside for a few days to see what America holds in her mountains. Backpacking has moved from being the sport of a select few to being a sport for millions. What is the reason for this growth?

There are, of course, numerous reasons to account for the incredible growth of backpacking as a popular sport. But of all the explanations, one stands out among all others.

That is, that backpacking represents an attempt by man to reintegrate himself with his environment. Man wants to see, smell and touch nature again. Modern urban life removes man from his natural environment and exposes him to an artificial setting of steel, concrete and glass.

It is possible for people to live for days, weeks and even years without ever seeing a blade of grass or a tree. The amount of nature that most people are exposed to consists of the trimmed lawns of suburbia, the crabgrass of an empty lot, or the controlled environment of a city park. For the vast majority of Americans, this represents their average exposure to nature over the course of the year. While we all enjoy the convenience and stability of modern urban living, people are more and more beginning to realize that the controlled environment of our urban areas deprives us of something. Call that something what you will; wanderlust, adventure, karma, or sensitivity. Any way you label it, it all comes down to one thing, the experiencing of nature. The ersatz environment of our cities deprives us of this experience. It is the deprivation of this experience that either consciously or unconsciously drives people to flee the city every summer.

The summertime ritual of fleeing the cities takes many forms. Some persons bivouac in the campsites of our national recreation areas. Some persons seek nature in country retreats. Some take to the waters and pit their skills against the wiles of nature's fish. Some persons find nature's tranquility exploring the roads and byways of America's undeveloped areas. Then, there are those who seek nature in the purest, most intimate form. These are they who would dare to expose themselves to nature's elements and animals. They venture beyond the domain of mankind, a domain where man and his machines, and his dams, and his disinfectants rule. They venture back to an era in time when man lacked the machines and shelters which now insulate him from mother earth.

This, then, is the world of the backpacker. For backpacking provides the urban man with one of the only ways of experiencing nature in her totality. Indeed, it is perhaps the finest way to experience Mother Nature.

Nature in her virgin state retains a tranquility not to be found in the man-made environment. It is this atmosphere of tranquility and purity that the backpacker seeks. For in it he finds himself and his soul. In the wilderness, urban man is able to reclaim an individuality and a sensitivity too often unattainable by him in his everyday life.

In our modern urban world man is often forced to define himself not as an individual but as a unit of a larger social mechanism. The wilderness experience allows us to redefine ourselves as individual, unique human beings. In a sense, then, backpacking as a sport represents one of the last bastions of individualism in a mass society.

While this quest for nature is the most important reason why people go backpacking, there are countless others.

Some persons set off on wilderness trails to test their physical stamina. The mountains offer them a challenge. Mountain passes and mountain peaks present goals to be challenged and conquered.

Some come to the mountains to seek specialized information on plants, rocks, and fauna. Botanists come to collect samples or to photograph plants unavailable in a garden. Biologists come to trace the movements and habitats of fish and game animals.

Others come merely to enjoy the serenity of the wilderness, with no other goal or object to their visit. This is the most common variety of backpacker. Such a person rarely has the great reserves of strength with which to conquer high summits. He may have no intense desire to challenge nature, nor does he possess a great deal of knowledge about biology and ecology. The average backpacker could be any person on the street. The only thing that differentiates him from any other person is that he wants to find out what is out there in the wilds. He is an explorer. He is the modern counterpart of the mighty mountain men who left the comforts of the eastern cities in the early eighteen hundreds to explore the then uncharted western United States. The backpacker of the nineteen seventies shares a common desire with these illustrious figures of a former day. He too seeks, for at least a short time, to break away from the fetters that bind him to society. In doing so the backpacker regains that part of himself that tells him to run away, away to a place where the world's cares will not touch him, to places where there exists beauty not to be found in a city: to the wilderness.

This desire to break away and seek the adventurous life of a wilderness backpacker is by no means a universal desire. While previously it was stated that people of all ages are physically capable of backpacking, not everyone is emotionally disposed to it. The backpacker is a special breed. A backpacker is the kind of person who would rather *play* golf than watch it on television. He is the kind of person who would rather *hike* up to the top of a mountain than drive up to it. He is the kind of person who knows that life's most valued pleasures are not found in an easy chair or in front of a television set, but out in the world beyond his everyday environment.

The backpacker is the person who knows that the best tasting trout in the world was *caught by him,* and not served up to him in a restaurant. He is the person who knows that the most spectacular view is seen not from a mountain peak that he drove his automobile up, but from the summit of a peak that he hiked up.

In short, he is a person who has not been seduced by our contemporary "civilization" to a state of atrophy. He is still somewhat of a "wild man," but in being so, he is more civilized than the so-called "modern man." For he still retains a sensitivity to the natural environment. This then is the backpacker. This is you.

You are the person for whom this book was written—a person who has either never tried backpacking, or has tried it but seeks to learn more. This book is an attempt to familiarize you, the reader, with the wilderness environment and some of the things that *you* can do to make your venture into it more enjoyable.

In the following chapters I have sought to offer recommendations that will maximize your comfort and enjoyment. At times the reader might find such recommendations sissified. This may indeed be true to some readers, but it is my philosophy that a trip is only as successful as its preparation. Proper preparation and use of adequate equipment can greatly enhance one's enjoyment of a wilderness outing. Conversely, inadequate planning and use of inferior equipment can make one so miserable that he will never again return to the wilderness. Thus, the best advice that I can give to novice backpackers is to plan carefully and to not shortcut suggestions.

Shearer

CHAPTER 2

EQUIPMENT

A backpacker's equipment is to him what tools are to a carpenter. In either case it would be extremely difficult to do a good job without the necessary equipment. In a similar sense, a carpenter knows that the work he does is only as good as his tools. Poor tools mean poor work to a carpenter. Poor equipment means hardship and aggravation to the backpacker.

Like the carpenter, the experienced backpacker knows that good equipment is not always cheap.

To those who would scoff at the above statement, let me give this example. Any carpenter knows that he can buy a screwdriver in a dime store for thirty-nine cents. Nevertheless he will invariably go to a hardware store and buy one costing many times more. Why? Because he knows that the costlier screwdriver is made of a drop forged alloy that will not crack or bend when put under great pressure. He knows without even looking that the thirty-nine cent screwdriver will break or bend the first time he puts it to hard use.

In a similar sense, an experienced backpacker knows that a cheap pair of shoes or a cheap sleeping bag is no bargain. A bargain-priced sleeping bag is no bargain if it cannot keep you warm. An equipment failure on an extended wilderness trip can be a great deal more serious to the backpacker than a simple broken screwdriver to a carpenter. A broken backpack can mean several days of sore shoulders, and an inferior pair of trail shoes may cause a bad fall with broken bones as the result. Some backpacking equipment can, of course, be compromised. It makes little difference what kind of shirt you wear, or what kind of socks you use. Failures of such equipment have little consequence, and their discussion here is of little concern.

The next three sections deal with three items of backpacking equipment which cannot be substituted for by inferior products. When it comes to selecting these three items—shoes, backpacks, and sleeping bags—quality should not be compromised. Experienced backpackers purchase these items with the care that a mountain climber uses in purchasing his climbing ropes.

As a rule, these items are not cheap. The cost of the three items will come to about $125, which seems quite steep. But beyond this single capital outlay, the backpacker-to-be will incur few expenses. If carefully chosen according to the specifications set forth in the following chapters, these items will, with proper care, last many years. The author presently owns a five-year-old backpack, an eight-year-old sleeping bag, and a four-year-old pair of hiking boots. None of these items shows any significant amount of wear and all should be usable for many years to come.

Quality equipment is durable, comfortable, and requires a minimum of maintenance. It is always well worth its premium price.

This revelation should not in any way discourage the beginning backpacker on a budget. To accommodate those on tight finances, suggestions are given on how to get started with practically nothing and only a few dollars outlay. But these short-cuts are not intended for those planning an extended back country trip. They are for the weekend jaunt, or an overnight trip. A hiker may safely lose one night's sleep in an inadequate sleeping bag, but ten such nights will tax the energy and strength of an Atlas. Similarly, a pair of sore shoulders resulting from carrying Uncle Harry's World War II knapsack is no great loss as long as they hurt for only one day. Top quality equipment is a must if one is going to enjoy the wilderness.

I have seen people in the back country with nothing more than a bag of dried seeds and a blanket. None of these people could convince me that they were enjoying themselves. An intelligent backpacker plans his trip carefully, uses good equipment, and enjoys himself. Follow this advice and have fun.

Shoes and Foot Care

The most important item on any backpacking trip will be your shoes. Unless you are experienced or know that you have very tough feet, a good pair of trail boots is a must. In no circumstances should street shoes be taken on a back-country trip. The smooth soles on street shoes are an invitation to disaster on smooth rock.

Many hikers set off for the high country with nothing but a pair of sneakers. Sneakers have the advantage of being very light, and they dry quickly. They also have the disadvantages of weak arch support and poor wearability. They can and do break up under trail conditions. The pliability of the soles can be a real disadvantage when traveling over rocky trails. Most persons' feet are not tough enough to wear sneakers under such conditions. Possibly for this reason, sneaker wearers seem to acquire many more blisters than those wearing good trail shoes. Still, many back countrymen wear them, and do so successfully. I would recommend them only for trips of short duration.

For the vast majority of us, who are endowed with feet of lesser toughness, a good pair of hiking boots is in order.

They should be of good construction. A sturdily made boot will last many years. It is not unusual to see hikers with boots that are ten years old. When buying a hiking boot, remember that a cheap pair is not necessarily a bargain if it will break apart on the trail. A lined boot, while costing more than an unlined boot, will last longer because two layers of leather take the strain instead of just one. A lined boot will also give your foot better support.

The most popular trail shoes are ankle high. Hikers have discovered over the years that the so-called "hunting boots" which extend up higher than the ankle are a poor choice. Such "high boots" restrict the length of your stride, can cause excessive chafing on your ankles, and tend to restrict blood circulation to the foot. High boots also mean that you will be carrying unnecessary extra weight. Lower boots allow the ankle to pivot freely, and tend to be more comfortable when worn for long periods.

The weight of the boot is also of some consideration. At the end of a long day a heavy boot will really make your feet drag. Consequently, some effort should be spent in finding a light boot. This tends to run counter to the idea of a well constructed boot. The logic here is that a boot cannot be both light and sturdily constructed. This need not be the case. There are many fine trail boots which weigh less than four pounds. And with a little looking, women should be able to find a lined boot with a good sole weighing about three pounds. This compares favorably with men's street shoes, which weigh about two pounds. The extra weight of a hiking boot is accounted for by the heavier grade of leather used in its construction, and the extra weight of the hiking sole.

The sole of a hiking shoe is very important, and must suit the terrain that is anticipated. A cushion rubber sole may be adequate for work shoes but is a poor choice for a hiking sole. Unless one is traveling mainly on packed dirt or sand, such soles are inadequate. Cushion rubber soles have minimal adhesion on moist surfaces and rock. Most mountain backpacking in the west is done on rocky trails. The best soles for such travel are composition lug soles. Perhaps the best sole of this type is the *Vibram Montagna.* It has very good wearability, and has incredible adhesion to smooth rock surfaces even when wet. This sole is also sold separately by mountain shops, and more recently in shoe repair shops. A pair of these soles can turn a comfortable pair of work shoes into hiking boots for a modest investment.

Two other factors to consider when looking for a hiking boot are the toe and the tongue. The toe should be reinforced so that it is either solid or extremely stiff. It is not unusual for a rock to flip over onto your toe, and this area is best protected. The tongue should be padded or at least be double-thickness leather. A plain single-thickness tongue has a tendency to "bunch up" during hiking. This can cause painful blisters. Also, the tongue should be attached to the body of the boot inside the lacing eyes. This prevents you from getting a "wet foot" should you step into a stream. It also prevents pebbles and dirt from getting inside.

When trying on a new pair of boots or checking out an old pair for trail use, make sure that your heel does not "ride up." If it does, the boot is too big. The heel of your foot should sit firmly in the boot. The toes should be somewhat loose, but not so much that the balls of your feet ride sloppily in the boot. Often the addition of an insole will improve the fit of an otherwise sloppy boot.

Many hikers have elaborate systems developed for wearing socks. Some wear one pair, some two, some three. Some wear their socks inside out. Some wear cotton under and wool over. Some wear nylon under, cotton over. Some wear only white socks, some wear only colored socks. All hikers proclaim their method the best. It is this author's contention that it does not really make much difference. Even if you have the most elaborate method of wearing socks, it will not make one iota of difference if your boots do not fit. You will still get blisters. So the best advice is, use any old system of socks (except holey ones), but just get *boots* that fit!

How does one get new boots to fit? Simply wear them. Too often a hiker takes off on a trip with a new pair of boots. The inevitable result is a pair of blistered feet. To avoid this fate, wear your new boots enough to thoroughly "break 'em in" before hitting the trail.

Unfortunately, the exigencies of modern life more often lead us to buy our boots a few days before we are to leave on that week-long trip. Fear not, for there is one quick way to "break em in" before leaving. But as with any quick method, it is not the most comfortable.

Start by soaking those beautiful new boots in water for a few minutes. Then put them on and start walking. They should mold themselves to your feet in an hour or so. Then just dry them out. Be sure to dry them slowly, not in front of a heater. Then rub them down with saddle soap, and they are ready to go.

You will notice that the boots must be dried *slowly*. This cannot be overemphasized. If dried quickly, leather becomes "cooked" and brittle. The fibrous matter is broken down, thus reducing the useful life of the boot. In no circumstances should boots be put close to a campfire to dry. If boots do not dry naturally and are still wet in the morning, just put them on with a dry pair of socks. Change socks if they get wet, and keep changing socks until the boot dries out. This same system should be used should you fall into a stream during the day. Change socks, especially if your feet are wet and cold. It is amazing to find how fast your feet will warm up if you put on dry socks, even if your boots are soaked.

Your boots are more likely to treat you kindly if you treat them kindly. After a trip, clean and polish (wax) them. This simple treatment will greatly extend the useful life of your boots. A simple waxing will make your boots quite repellent to water; so will oiling your boots. But oiling is frowned upon by some hikers because it has a tendency to soften the leather. The logic here is that if the leather is softened, it will stretch out of shape. Another measure used by some hikers to waterproof their boots is to paint the seams with a silicone or wax sealant. At least one of these measures, including waxing, should be used in caring for your boots. Such care will keep them dry and comfortable on the trail.

Pounding ten miles of mountain trail under your feet every day is not the best care that can be given to those appendages. Nevertheless, most people's feet can readily tolerate the stress placed on them, and with a little care they will pull through without causing you too much discomfort.

The two greatest enemies to your feet will be friction and moisture. Friction is best taken care of by getting a well fitted pair of broken-in boots. The moisture is a more complicated matter.

Moisture is caused mostly by sweating of your feet or by a dunk in a mountain stream. This moisture inside your boots softens the skin, making it far more susceptible to blistering. Tough dry skin resists the rubbing friction of the boot. Soft moist skin will tend to move more with the motion of the shoe. If the difference in motion between the shoe and the foot is great, the layers of skin on the foot will separate and create a blister. Thus, one of the best ways to prevent blisters is to keep your feet as *dry* as possible. This is best done by taking off the shoes and socks at lunchtime, and perhaps during an afternoon rest break. If the socks are still wet when it is time to go, break out a dry pair. It is also a good practice to soak your feet in a cold stream at lunchtime for a few minutes. The stream will cool them, and the quick drying afterwards seems to toughen the skin. It is truly amazing how refreshing this soaking is for tired feet!

The moisture and heat inside your boots make ideal conditions for a case of athlete's foot. Proper ventilation of your feet and frequent changes of socks should provide adequate protection. If no one in the group with which you are traveling has athlete's foot to begin with, you are probably safe for the trip. Some backpackers use foot powders, but they probably do so more out of habit than need. Unless someone has athlete's foot, powders are just as well left behind. They will not keep your feet dry under trail conditions. Your feet will be giving off too much moisture for them to be effective.

Lacing your boots properly is all important. Lace them as tightly as possible and make sure that the knot does not slip. If you find the knot slipping, put a drop of spittle on it. In most cases it will stop slipping.

Lacing tightly is always important, but is especially important on downhill stretches. Always stop and tighten up your laces before downhill stretches. Doing this will prevent blisters. To understand this, one needs only to visualize the motion of your feet inside your boots as you walk downhill.

When your forward foot lands on the ground in a downhill stride, it is not only carrying the entire load of you and your pack, but also the extra load of that weight being accelerated downhill by gravity. Furthermore, you do not have the solid counter of your heel to absorb the shock. The tendency is for the foot to slip forward on the downstep. The foot then reseats itself to the back when lifted up. Unless minimized by lacing the boots tightly, this forward-back motion will lead to the swift formation of blisters on the toes and balls of the feet. Such extra care is not necessary on uphill stretches, but even here the boots should be firmly laced.

Should you start to feel sore spots or blisters, *stop immediately,* and take off your boot and sock. Continuing travel will result in a bigger blister or changing of a sore spot into a blister.

In the case of blisters, most authorities, including the U.S. Army and the American National Red Cross, approve of opening and draining the affected area. But they caution you to clean and sterilize the area as thoroughly as possible before piercing the blister. Unfortunately, it is not always possible to thoroughly wash and sterilize the affected area on the trail. A good substitute for soap and water is to clean the area with a Wash-n-Dri towelette. Carry a few with you for this purpose.

After cleaning the area, hold a pin, needle, or knife point under a match for a few seconds. This will sterilize it. Then prick a small hole in the blister near the edge, and drain it onto a handkerchief or facial tissue. It is important that you prick only a small hole in the blister. A large hole may cause the skin to slough off prematurely. It is better to leave the dead outer skin alone and let it slough off by itself. Premature removal slows the growth of the new skin and invites infection.

It is at this point that treatment of blisters and raw spots becomes a point of contention. Most medical authorities recommend the use of an absorbent dressing or moleskin over the blister. Many experienced hikers merely slap a piece of adhesive tape directly on the blister. If this latter course is chosen, do not remove the tape for at least five days. Doing so beforehand will result in the dead skin being pulled away prematurely. The logic in merely putting a piece of adhesive tape directly on the wound is that the cause of the blister or sore spot is usually from excessive movement and pressure on the spot. Putting thick bandages on it merely increases the pressure and therefore is less comfortable than plain adhesive tape. Another possible way is to put a thin ridge of adhesive tape on four sides of the blister, thus keeping it from contact with the shoe. Put a band-aid or another adhesive over the top.

Finally, do not wear your socks to bed at night. Your socks will be moist and dirty. The moisture will soften your feet and could cause a case of athlete's foot. Generally your feet will be the last area of your body to warm up at night, so just relax and wait. If they still do not warm up, push a dry shirt down into your sleeping bag to give them some extra cover.

Backpacks

Except for your shoes, the most important item of equipment will be your backpack. For those whose only experience with backpacks was the Army, it should be pointed out that the old rucksack and Army packboard have been superseded by modern-style backpacks. These modern-style "packs" consist of an aluminum (or magnesium) frame which contours itself to the body. Upon this a canvas or nylon bag is suspended. For anyone contemplating anything more than a weekend outing, such a unit is a must.

For those who do not own a modern-style backpack or those who own an admittedly poor one, I would strongly recommend the purchase of a good-quality backpack. A top-quality unit will last many years and will stand up under abuse that an inferior backpack would break under.

Do not take off on a week-long outing with an old knapsack which was meant to carry a picnic lunch. Either your shoulders or the knapsack will give out on you. If you cannot afford the purchase of a top-quality backpack, borrow one from a friend, or rent one. Many sport shops now rent excellent backpacks for modest rates. For those who do not know which brand to buy, or those who do not know if they will like backpacking enough to warrant the purchase of a backpack, renting provides a good alternative.

There are presently about five manufacturers of modern-style contour-frame backpacks in the United States. Some of these manufacturers produce good units. Some provide only mediocre quality. Since all of these units operate on the same principles of weight distribution, there are certain common characteristics by which one can evaluate the quality of a backpack. Since this is the case, let us look at those characteristics which make a good backpack:

1. The backpack should have a fully welded frame which contours to your back. The more crossframes (horizontal frames) the unit has, the better. Some backpacks have as many as five.

2. All shoulder straps and hip bands should be fully adjustable. The more adjustments that can be made both on the straps and on the frame, the better. Most of the better brands have at least two sets of points for attaching the shoulder straps at the shoulders, and some have two sets at the hips. This is important for youngsters whose growth will otherwise render a big investment useless.

3. All shoulder straps and hip bands should be padded, and the padding should not have a strap running through it. If it does, it is virtually useless. The purpose

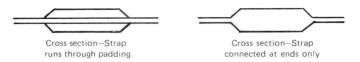

Cross section—Strap   Cross section—Strap
runs through padding   connected at ends only

of a padded strap is to distribute the load. If the strap runs through the pad, there is no load distribution. A properly made shoulder or hip pad distributes the load by placing an ensolite or polyurethane pad within a wide strip of tubular nylon. The strap or grommet is then attached at the extremities of this pad. If you do not want a case of sore shoulders, buy only a backpack with straps made this way.

4. Backbands (bands running across the frame that bear against your back) should be adjustable. They may have to be tightened or moved to a different position, on the trail. They should be at least five inches wide. Those with turnbuckle adjustment are best. Padding on the backband can also be desirable.

5. The best backpacks have the packbag connected to the packframe by means of grommets and clevis pins through the packframe. Some bags are still made which "hang" on the frame by means of a sock-like arrangement over the vertical bars of the frame. It has been my personal experience that these socks break through, and other lashings must then be improvised. This may not sound so bad, but can be a nuisance on the trail where repair materials are not readily available.

6. Last, the bag itself should have a suspension frame. This holds the load close to your back where it belongs. Without one, the load sags outward away from your back, giving rise to the "rucksack syndrome" wherein you must bend forward excessively to compensate for the load pulling back.

Adjusting the Frame to Fit

About two out of every three backpackers that you meet on the trail will be wearing ill-fitting packs. Their shoulders will be sagging, their backs aching, and their spirits drooping, all unnecessarily.

If you are going into the wilderness to enjoy nature, you should be doing just that, not worrying about your aching shoulders. Unless you are a masochist, there is no reason why you should be worrying about the pain in your back instead of enjoying the beautiful country around you. It would be fallacious to say that you will experience no discomfort at all from a properly fitted backpack. Even a well fitted pack can leave you with a stiff neck and sore hips at the end of a hard day. Still, you should not be noticeably uncomfortable while you are on the trail.

The first step in getting a comfortable backpack is selecting one that can be adjusted to your physique. The most important dimension here is the distance between shoulders and hips. Bear this in mind when you go to your local sport shop to buy your backpack. When you have selected a backpack, have the salesman put twenty to forty pounds of weight in it, depending on whether you are a woman or a man. Most stores have sand bags especially on hand for this purpose. This is a more effective method of simulating a loaded pack than merely having someone press the pack downward. The latter method does not let you walk around the store to see how the pack will set on your back when you are walking.

Put the pack on your back and strap the waistband around your hips. Remember, the waistband should carry eighty to ninety percent of the weight. Pull it tight, as it should be fitted relatively tight on the trail. Women should fit the waistband where they feel it will be most comfortable with the load, keeping in mind that the band will chafe the skin where bones are not padded with a layer of fat. Men should be careful not to wear the waistband so low that it interferes with leg movement.

Next check the shoulder straps. They should be pulled tight so that the backbands of the packframe are touching your back. The shoulder straps should be attached to the frame at a point at least one inch higher than the highest point on your shoulders. This is the most critical measurement in fitting the backpack to you. If the point of attachment is too low, the weight will rest not on your hips but on your shoulders.

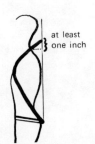

at least one inch

Do not lose faith if the shoulder straps ride a little bit too low, for there is an adjustment which you can make. Most manufacturers and their dealers who set up the units attach the shoulder straps from the

 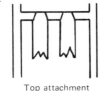

bottom of the cross bar. By removing the "O" ring and clevis pin, and then reattaching the shoulder straps from the *top* of the cross bar, you can raise

Bottom attachment   Top attachment

the point at which the shoulder straps are attached to the frame about three-quarters of an inch. Thereby you will also be increasing the distance between that point and the highest point on your shoulders.

This seemingly insignificant distance can make a world of difference to your physical comfort on the trail. If the shoulder straps are level with or below the level of your shoulders (Diagram A), the weight of the pack will rest either entirely or at least significantly on your shoulders. This defeats the entire purpose of the modern backpack. If you carry your backpack thus,

you might as well have bought a World War II rucksack at an Army surplus store for a couple of dollars. Modern backpacks are made to carry the weight of the load on your hips. Experience has shown this to be the most comfortable and efficient way for humans to carry loads. This concentration of weight on the hips can be accomplished only if the shoulder straps are attached to the frame above the level of the shoulders (diagram B).

Another occurrence discovered while fitting backpacks is that the straps are often set too high above the shoulders (diagram C). If the distance to the point where the shoulder straps are attached is more than three inches above the shoulders, the pack will wobble sidewise as you walk. This would tend to indicate that the pack frame is too big for you. A smaller frame is better unless you can (1) raise the point at which the waistband is attached or (2) lower the point at which the shoulder straps are attached. Several of the better backpacks enable you to do this. Such adjustable backpacks are excellent for growing children.

Last, check the backbands, especially the lower one. The lower backband will be carrying much of the weight of the pack. Be sure when you tighten up the waistband that you cannot feel the lower crossbar touching your rear. If you can feel it now, you will really feel it on the trail. Your next step is to pull the backband down on the frame, or just tighten it up. Also be careful that during the trip the backband does not slip upward on the frame, thus exposing your posterior to the chafe of the crossbar. If it slips up, pull it down and tighten it up. It should be mentioned here that some of the better packs have special ties which prevent the backband from creeping up on the frame.

It is my opinion that if the reader adjusts his backpack according to these instructions, a minimum of discomfort can be expected on the trail.

Packing

Properly organizing your packbag makes things easier to get at. You do not have to rummage through everything to find "that bandaid" while everyone else waits for you. Furthermore, a properly packed bag is easier to carry.

A good backpacker will pack his bag using the identical pattern every day. This way he can go directly to whatever he needs without rummaging around. Decide on a pattern and stick to it.

Also, use an uncompartmented bag. You can pack at least ten percent more into an uncompartmented bag. Compartments are frills. By forcing you to put certain things above or below, they do not give you a well balanced pack. As for convenience, if you have your food in one bag, your toiletries in another, and odds and ends in the outside pockets, you will never be inconvenienced.

Weight distribution is of utmost importance in packing your backpack. The old rucksack held the weight low and away from the back. To counterbalance the tendency of the load to throw him on his back, an individual had to bend forward. Modern backpacks are designed so that the weight will be held high and close to your back. This eliminates the need to bend forward excessively as with the old rucksack.

OLD   MODERN
RUCKSACK   PACK

By packing your bag properly, you will be rewarded with a comfortably fitting pack and a minimum of bending over on the uphill stretches. To this end, care should be taken to keep the heavy items high and against your back (diagram A). Light items should be packed in the lower part of the unit (diagram C). Weight in this area will cause you to bend forward excessively on uphill and flat stretches. It is for this reason that sleeping bags are usually carried down low. Being light, this is the best place to carry them.

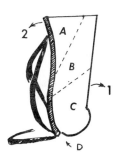

The reason for this distribution is readily visualized in the diagram. All weight in the backpack is focused on pivot point "D," the point where the waistband is attached. If extra weight is placed on area "C," the tendency of the backpack will be to pull the load backward (1) away from the back. The only way to compensate for this tendency is to lean forward more (2) to balance the load.

Since the object of the modern packframe is to let you stand straight up and walk more comfortably, do not pack a liter of canned fuel in the bottom outside part of the bag. A good rule to remember is "heavies high, lights low.", It will save you from lumbago.

Plastic bags are now universally accepted among backpackers as the best medium in which to carry things inside the packbag. They are lightweight, waterproof, dustproof, and shock resistant.

Food (which will be discussed later) should always be put in a plastic bag, as should first-aid supplies. Other things are optional, but some backpackers put everything in plastic, including tents, clothes, sleeping bags and matches. This may sound foolish, but these persons are completely sure that their gear will be dry, even if they themselves are soaked to the skin by rain or an accidental slip in a stream.

Packing should be done carefully and sensibly. For instance, do not carry a tube tent on top and your canteen in the bottom of the packbag. Consider an item's use and place it appropriately. Extra clothes and down parkas belong on the bottom of the pack during the day.

A final hint. If toward the end of a trip you find the bag section of your pack only half full (you probably ate the other half), put your sleeping bag in the packbag. By leaving a void at the bottom of the frame, you will be raising the weight of the load higher onto the frame. Thus readjusting the weight, you will not have to lean forward as much, and the unit will consequently be easier to carry. It should be pointed out, however, that this makes for a less stable arrangement and should not be done if one is traveling difficult terrain or crossing many streams.

Sleeping Bags

Getting a good night's sleep out on the trail is very important. A hard day of trail pounding will exhaust all but the supermen among us. To get a good night's sleep it is necessary that you sleep in something that will keep you warm. If you cannot get warm at night, you are not going to get your strength back for the next day. Consequently, carrying a good sleeping bag with you is of utmost importance.

In the last five years, down-filled nylon sleeping bags have become the universal choice of backpackers. They are light, warm, and compact. A good down bag with two pounds of prime goose down will weigh about three to three and a half pounds and will keep a person warm down to about 30°F. A bag of equivalent warmth, using Dacron ® as a filler, will weigh about twice as much, Fiberfill II®, 1½ times as much.

A sleeping bag's warmth is determined by the amount of air that can be trapped in the filler material. This dead air forms an insulation barrier between your body and the cold air outside, and retains your body's warmth inside the bag.

Goose down has been found to trap more air on a pound-for-pound basis than any other material. This is primarily a result of its resiliency.

If you are considering the purchase of a down sleeping bag, several things should be considered, especially if you intend to use the bag for backpacking. First, what kind of bag do you want, a mummy bag or a traditional rectangular bag? Mummy bags are the warmest on a pound-for-pound basis, but they are confining. If you think that you can get used to the confinement, it is a better purchase. Rectangular bags, on the other hand, will be more comfortable because you can move around in them, but they weigh more because of the added area to be insulated.

Construction of the bag is also very important. Always be sure that the inner and outer covers are not sewn through. Such construction except in the case of some specialty products is to be avoided. A bag of "box" style construction is best for backpacking. This design consists of

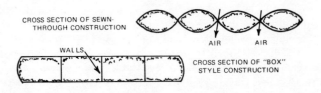

CROSS SECTION OF SEWN-THROUGH CONSTRUCTION

AIR   AIR

WALLS

CROSS SECTION OF "BOX" STYLE CONSTRUCTION

what appears to be a series of boxes lined up together. Actually, walls of fabric are sewn between the inner and outer envelopes. These walls hold the inner and outer envelopes apart, thus preventing cold air from leaking in as with the sewn-through design. The box-style design allows the down to loft (fluff) more than any other design, and is the construction lightest in weight for the warmth it offers.

Still, down does have two drawbacks. First, it does not loft well when it gets wet. If it will not loft, it will not trap air and warm up. Thus, on long trips it is a smart idea to carry your bag in a plastic sack to prevent it from getting wet in a rain or in an accidental dunk in a stream.

Second, down sleeping bags do not insulate you from the ground underneath. Thus, it is usually necessary to carry a pad with you to do this job. And do not forget that the pad will weigh something. Most backpackers use the popular ensolite pads. Others use foam rubber or urethane pads, and a few use air mattresses, which are heavy and bulky. Experience has shown this backpacker that all are adequate when the ground is not too cold, and none are adequate when it is. One winter night found me with two foam pads, one ensolite pad, two blankets, and one pair of pants under me, and my hips were still cold.

For these reasons, some backpackers prefer Dacron® or Fiberfill II® (Du Pont) as a filler material. Besides the fact that top quality synthetic-filled bags cost less than half as much as down-filled bags, they retain some of their warmth even when wet. Furthermore, under moderate conditions, an insulating pad is not usually needed with a good synthetic bag. While synthetic bags do not pack as neatly as down bags, most are not so bulky that they cannot be carried at the bottom of your pack frame.

If you own a synthetic-filled bag, check how much fill it has before you take it backpacking. A mummy bag should have at least 3 pounds of fill, and a rectangular bag should have no less than 3½ pounds of fill. A rectangular bag with less than 3½ pounds fill may be adequate on a weekend outing, but carry an extra wool blanket to be safe. You should never attempt an extended trip with a synthetic-filled bag having less than the aforementioned amounts of filler material.

In most circumstances, your bag will collect moisture given off by your body and condensed during the night. It is a good habit to hang up your bag in the morning sun or at lunchtime. This will air it out and dry up any moisture in it. Moisture will reduce the warmth of your bag; therefore, it is important that you keep it as dry as possible.

In drying it out, do not get carried away. Just hang it from a tree limb or lay it on a rock for an hour or so. In the summer sun, even a wet bag will dry in no time flat.

Tents

Backpackers' opinions on tents are as numerous as their personalities. Some persons would never set foot on a wilderness trail if they did not have a stand-up-inside tent with them. Then there are those rugged individualists who, in the spirit of John Muir, would not consider taking a tent with them even if a week-long rainstorm were anticipated.

Naturally, everyone has his own reason for taking or not taking a tent on a backpacking trip. Some reasons for taking a tent along are quite valid. Prominent among these reasons is that a tent offers the best possible rain protection. Getting caught out in the wilderness in a cold driving rainstorm is no fun, especially when such a storm strikes at night when you are trying to sleep.

One of the cardinal rules of backpacking is not to let your sleeping bag get wet. Wet sleeping bags, especially wet down sleeping bags, do not keep you warm. When down gets wet, it mats down, and thereby loses its insulating qualities. Consequently, if you get caught out in a rainstorm at night without a tent, it is absolutely necessary to put your sleeping bag away so that it does not get wet. It is evident that a rainstorm in such circumstances could mean a cold night sitting out in the rain. Having a tent in the same circumstances ensures you of a good night's sleep in a dry sleeping bag.

Another valid reason for taking a tent along is to protect you from the cold. While most backpacking is not done under extreme temperature conditions, it is not altogether uncommon for summertime temperatures to dip below freezing at night. A night under such temperature conditions should not bother a backpacker with a reasonably good sleeping bag. However, this situation can be drastically different if there is a substantial wind blowing.

No Wind   Heavy Wind

As we have seen in the previous section, the warmth of a sleeping bag is dependent upon the amount of air that can be trapped in the bag's insulating material. What was not mentioned is that the ability of the sleeping bag to keep the occupant warm is also dependent upon the amount of *warm* air trapped in that insulating material. Naturally, the body can give off only so much warmth to heat the air within the insulating material. As the warmth given off by the body distributes itself within the insulating material, some warmth will diffuse to the surface of the bag and be lost to the cold air outside the bag. Under normal windless conditions the amount of warmth lost from the surface of the bag is negligible. However, under cold, windy conditions, the amount of warm air lost from the bag's surface can be substantial enough to make the bag ineffective in keeping its occupant warm.

The principle operating here can be easily demonstrated by touching your tongue to your hand. Wait a few seconds in the still air, and you will feel a slight sensation of coolness. Then blow on it. The wet spot will feel distinctly cold. Your breath cools your hand in much the same way that the cold wind can cool your sleeping bag.

In most circumstances it is possible to protect your sleeping bag from the cold wind simply·by throwing a plastic sheet over your bag, or by setting up your bed behind a windbreak. Nevertheless, it is not uncommon to find oneself camped out on a windy plateau above the tree line without any windbreak. In such circumstances, a tent can add greatly to your sleeping bag's warmth. It should be pointed out here that the tent will *not* warm up inside significantly. It will be almost as cold inside the tent as outside. However, the tent will stop the movement of the cold air over your sleeping bag, and this factor will add to your warmth.

Still another reason for using a tent is to keep the insects away from you at night. As science has yet to develop an insect repellent that will keep the pesky bugs from bothering you (although science does have a repellent which will keep them from biting you), a nighttime retreat from the buzzing hoards can be a blessing. Insects buzzing around you all night can be very bothersome, especially during the early summer months. Furthermore, bites incurred while asleep can be numerous and painful.

Nighttime insect activity is most prevalent in areas characterized by high evening temperatures $(60°F+)$ and in places which are close to water or where the ground is moist.

Thus, we have seen the three primary reasons for carrying a tent: rain, cold winds, and insect protection. Naturally these factors will vary from time to time and place to place. For instance, a rain shelter of some sort is a virtual necessity on a week-long trip into the Washington Cascade range during June. On the other hand, one can go on a week-long trip into the Sierra of California during August virtually without rain protection and be reasonably sure of staying dry. Still, there are those who would go out in the Cascades for a week with only a poncho.

In any case, one should consider a couple of factors before he runs down to his local sport shop to buy a tent. A primary consideration is cost. A good tent is not cheap. Expect to spend $40 to $150 for a complete rig ready for backpacking. Also, remember that unless you have a pack animal to carry it, you will be bearing the extra load of the tent yourself. A good two-man tent weighs *at least* five pounds, complete. That is a lot of money to spend and a lot of pounds to carry around on your back if you do not really need to carry it.

If at all possible, try to avoid taking a tent. Tents are both bulky and heavy. It is nearly impossible to fold them back into the neat little bundle like they came from the manufacturer.

For those backpackers who do not expect to be exposed to prolonged or frequent rain, the plastic "tube tent" is the best compromise. A tube tent is no more than a large piece of lightweight plastic formed in the shape of a tube. When a cord is strung through the tube and tied off to two trees, a sort-of tent emerges which is impervious to rain.

A good two-man tube tent and fifty feet of quarter inch nylon cord can be purchased for as little as $4. Such a set-up weighs about three pounds (two-man size), and it can double as a ground cloth. Furthermore, if it tears you can throw it away and buy a new one without breaking your budget. For these reasons, the tube tent is gaining acceptance among more and more backpackers as the best solution to the shelter problem.

The only drawback to the tube tent is the problem of condensation inside when you sleep in it, a problem not found in the expensive type of shelter. This can be annoying if one's sleeping bag gets wet. But most mountain mornings beam clear and bright, so just turn the tube tent inside out and lay it on a big rock in the sun along with your sleeping bag, and they will both dry out while you fix breakfast.

If you must have a tent, at least get a good rig. A good tent must have enough room in it to get your packs inside it. A two-man tent is not a two-man tent if you can only get two men in it but not their gear. Test it before you buy it. Be sure that the floor material is "waterproof." The roof should be "water repellent," the difference being that the former is coated with a plastic material to make it impervious to water, but the latter is merely uncoated nylon which is treated with a silicone solution so that it repels water. Such water repellent roofs are porous enough to let water vapor out (i.e., from your breath at night), but should hold off a light sprinkle. If made water*proof,* the roof would not breathe, so condensation would occur as with the tube tent.

It should be noted that some of the latest tents are made not with water-repellent sides, but rather with lightweight untreated rip-stop nylon. Such tents must be used with a rain fly, and in anything more than a sprinkle are useless without it. My only objection to this arrangement is that the rain flies usually marketed with these tents do not carry the rain far enough away from the tent. Consequently, water runs under the tent, making a muddy mess when it is time to pick up camp.

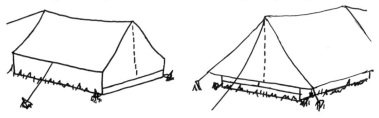

A good and cheap solution to this is not to buy the manufacturer's fancy rain fly, which usually costs $20-$25, but to get a piece of 12 by 12, three mil plastic, pound grommets in the corners and along the sides as tie-downs, and you are set. It will also double as a ground cloth when it's not raining.

Finally, if severe or prolonged rains are encountered dig a trench around your tent. A flat piece of shale or granite will work as a shovel in soft ground. Trenches do work and can keep the floor of your tent dry. Those who dig them are rarely sorry. If you do dig a trench, be sure to restore the ground to its natural state when you break camp.

CHAPTER 3

KEEPING IT LIGHT

In the previous chapter the reader has certainly noticed the emphasis placed on keeping equipment lightweight. The importance of this cannot be overemphasized. Even by using top-quality lightweight equipment, it is virtually impossible to go on a three-day trip with less than twenty pounds on your back. More often, the average backpacker will have far more than twenty pounds along. How much more is one of the backpacker's most important considerations. It might even be said that the enjoyment of one's day on the trail is in inverse proportion to how much he has to carry with him beyond his basic necessities.

An overburdened backpacker is not going to be a happy traveler. While it is possible for a man to carry sixty to seventy pounds on his back, his physical and emotional buoyancy will certainly be diminished. While some backpackers pride themselves on the size of their loads, such attitudes should be frowned upon. An intelligent backpacker keeps his load light. He does not overburden himself with frills or unneeded equipment.

Years of experience have shown that there are certain reasonable weight limits as to what one can comfortably carry on his back. A man of average weight can generally carry up to forty pounds comfortably. A woman of average weight can only carry about twenty pounds in comfort. Of course, in the comfort of your home you can say that these are unrealistically low estimates of your carrying capacity. But if you are of average build, these figures should be seriously viewed as being maximum weight limits for comfortable backpacking. Men should try to shoot for a load well under forty pounds, possibly close to thirty pounds. Women will be a little less flexible, but should nevertheless try to keep the load under twenty pounds. In either case, careful consideration of every item is necessary to keep weight down. To help the reader determine what sort of things deserve priority in his backpack, the balance of this chapter is given over to discussing those items of equipment not previously mentioned.

Each item is discussed separately, with careful consideration of its usefulness and weight.

Clothing is of first and foremost importance. Most novice backpackers are notoriously guilty of carrying too many clothes. It seems as though they have some kind of fear of "the dirt," and are constantly trying to stay in clean clothes. The best advice that I can give to such persons is to relax. Forget it. The dirt will not harm you. It is amazing how after a few days of camping out one hardly notices it. Extra clothes clutter up your pack and will cause more grief than comfort.

In moderate climates such as are found in most western mountain regions in the summer, take only what you will be wearing plus two extra pairs of socks, one change of underwear, a pair of shorts (women may prefer a skirt), a poncho or raincoat, and a jacket to shield you from the night's cold. There is only one conceivable circumstance in which more clothes should be carried, and that is expectation of cold or severe weather conditions.

Exceptionally dirty clothes can be partially washed with a bar of soap and then hung out on a tree to dry. They can also dry out during the day by hanging from your pack as you hike.

What is the best kind of clothes to take backpacking? Take only clothes which can stand the heavy abuse of outdoor living. Jeans are the standard. Take a pair that is not worn through, as a week out of doors can be hard on even a new pair. Also be sure that they are loose fitting and do not bind. New jeans should be washed and softened before use; otherwise they may chafe your thighs. On top, almost anything can be worn, but most backpackers prefer wool or wash-and-wear fabrics. Underneath, many prefer the fishnet-style underwear. Whatever you choose, be sure that it is comfortable.

Toiletries should also be chosen carefully, and should include only those things which are absolutely necessary. A basic list would consist of a toothbrush and paste, a comb, a bar of soap, a deodorant, a small towel, sun protection salves, and toilet paper. Women may find a hairbrush a necessity, but do not let the little lady get carried away with sprays, mouthwashes and cosmetics. The aforementioned kit should weigh about twelve ounces and should never amount to more than a pound. Weight can be saved by sharing some toiletries such as toothpaste, deodorant and soap. Another way to save weight is to put some cream deodorant (which usually comes in ridiculously heavy glass jars) into a small plastic pill vial.

I have come to prefer facial tissues over toilet paper, as they are softer, stronger, and more convenient for around-the-camp cleanups. Regardless of which you choose, plan to use it liberally, and use only white, not colored tissue. It has been found that the pigments used in colored bathroom tissue inhibit biodegradation of the cellulose fibers. In layman's terms, this means that colored tissue will not disintegrate unless burned, as Nature's little creatures (bacteria) will not eat colored tissue. Incidentally, if you plan on taking a roll of toilet paper, tear out the cardboard inner core and it will pack flatter.

Most men forget about shaving when out in the wilderness, but then again there are those that *must*. If you are one of those who will simply melt if you do not shave every morning, for heaven's sake do not take a can of lather along. Try making suds with plain soap and water over the fire. For electric shaver fans, there are several battery-operated shavers presently marketed in the U.S. All are quite good. As a final hint, use the same batteries in both your shaver and your flashlight should you choose to take one.

Matches are an obvious necessity and should be carefully shielded from moisture. A small waterproof cylinder is recommended, but adequate waterproofing can be provided by wrapping plain book matches inside several layers of plastic bag or plastic freezer wrap. If you are taking book matches, make several packets up in this form to be safe. Also, it is a good idea to place book matches in every pocket and container in your packbag. They weigh almost nothing, and save you the fuss of poking all around for them when needed.

First-aid kits, maps and *compass* should always be given priority consideration in loading up your packbag for a trip. These items will be discussed later.

A *knife* can be a very useful item for cleaning fish and a hundred other odd tasks. Other tasks might include cutting tent cord, opening plastic bags, cleaning fingernails, opening cans, and cutting adhesive tape. Most backpackers take one along. Those who do not bring a knife usually wish they had.

Like knives, *canteens* are the sort of item that most persons take along, and those who do not, regret it.

Water is abundant in the early summer in nearly all mountain ranges in the western United States with the possible exception of a few ranges in the southwest. Thus, the apparent need for a canteen is minimal. Nevertheless, hiking in the high mountains can rapidly drain your body of water in the form of sweat, and thirst can come on fast and strong. In some cases, you will find that only a few minutes after you have crossed a stream, you become thirsty. Such a circumstance can be very uncomfortable if it is still a long climb over the next ridge to another stream. The presence of a canteen will quickly alleviate your thirst. Its absence will mean great discomfort.

In late summer, never go without a canteen. Streams that are otherwise full of water can be bone dry in September and October. One September, a friend and I hiked fully eight miles to a stream which on arrival proved to be dry except for a pool of muddy larva-infested water. With parched throats, we had to wait for another half hour until we were sure that the iodine tablets had done their work. While we had canteens with us, we had foolishly left them empty at the start of the day's trek.

That taught us another lesson: keep your canteen full. This is especially true on late summer wilderness trips when streams are very likely to be empty. If you are backpacking earlier in the summer when the streams are fuller, examine the map of the trail ahead every morning in order to determine the need to carry water and how much. It is a good rule to always carry a pint for every two persons.

Water weighs about two pounds per quart, so do not go around carrying a full two-quart canteen unless it is deemed necessary. A simple look at the map in the morning will reveal your need to carry more than the standard pint.

I prefer taking two one-quart canteens to one two-quart canteen. This arrangement is much more convenient at mealtimes. It permits you to mix drinks in one canteen while leaving the other canteen full of fresh water for cooking.

I also prefer transparent plastic canteens to aluminum canteens. They are easier to clean, and do not seem to hold the flavor and odor of what was previously inside the canteen. Metal canteens occasionally react with the substance inside and leave the metal pitted. This makes cleaning difficult and provides a haven for bacteria. The substances used to make plastic canteens are nearly inert (i.e., they do not react with foods). Consequently, pitting cannot occur, thus giving you a more hygienic container. Furthermore, the smooth, nonreactive quality of plastic makes the containers easier to clean and makes flavors and odors less likely to adhere to their surfaces.

On a wilderness outing, the dividing line between a necessity and a luxury becomes nearly impossible to define. In reality, it is more a matter of personal taste than objective fact. To demonstrate this point, let us use the following examples.

Matches, to use an ideal example, would probably be viewed as an absolute necessity by 100% of all backpackers, but a *canteen* might be seen as a necessity by only 80% of backpackers. A *hat* might be viewed in this light by fewer yet. Thus, individual desires and an eye to keeping the weight of your backpack down will be your best guides in deciding what to take. With this in mind, the reader is invited to scrutinize those items mentioned beyond this point as being helpful but not necessary aids to the backpacker.

The use of a *flashlight* is considered the criterion which separates the old timer from, the young whippersnapper. The old timer would not be caught dead with one. If you feel the need of a flashlight—and one often does come in handy—buy one which uses two AA batteries. This is the most convenient and lightweight size for a backpack trip. A couple of fresh alkaline batteries should easily last through a ten-day trip.

Sunglasses are practically a necessity on a summer wilderness trip. Summer sunshine in the high mountains can be very intense. While it is very unlikely that you will suffer eye damage from the sun, you will be much more comfortable with a good pair of sunglasses. Squinting all day can become very annoying to those who do not heed this advice.

It pays to get a good pair of prescription or optically perfect glasses, as you will be wearing them for about eight hours a day. The second best alternative to this is to buy a pair of polarized sun glasses. These glasses reduce glare better than nonpolarized glasses and are well worth their price.

If you wear contact lenses, leave them at the trail head. Dirt particles from the trail have an uncanny way of finding their way underneath the lenses. After washing them ten times a day, you will wish that you had left them at home. Take your spectacles, with a pair of clip-on

Polaroid sunglasses. If your lenses are not safety glass, better take an extra pair along.

Finally, if you wear any kind of glasses whatsoever, it is a good idea to have some sort of *retaining cord* around the back of the glasses to prevent them from slipping off should you fall or trip.

One luxury which persons frequently go overboard on is photographic equipment. Take only one *camera* along. One camera can adequately take care of all the needs of as many as four people. The only exception to this would be if a group planned on splitting into two groups to hike on alternate routes during the day. Needless to say, tripods are to be avoided unless photography is the sole purpose of the trip. The mountains are littered with natural tripods—rocks. Place your camera equipment in a handy outside pocket so that you don't have to fumble for it when you want it.

Books provide an excellent diversion from the day's activities, as do diaries. Paperback books are the obvious favorites because of weight. Favorite topics of backpackers include naturalist studies and the writings of John Muir. Books also provide an excellent diversion on layover days when you are not hiking. They allow you to while away the day with a lack of exertion, totally involved in your own little world. Books also provide a good change of pace from your companions' conversation. An average paperback weighs only about six to eight ounces, and it is well worth every ounce.

A *watch* can be a great asset in planning out your day. Most backpackers organize their day around the rising and setting of the sun. But it is hard for even an experienced backpacker to tell what time it is by the sun, and after it goes down, there is no way to tell the hour of the day unless you are an expert at telling stars. A watch can tell you when it is time to go to bed, when to get up, and when to stop hiking and make camp for the night. This last point is especially important, as it is difficult to cook a meal in the dark, not to mention cleaning up. A watch also lets you gauge your pace, especially when traveling over relatively featureless terrain. For instance, if you know that you can travel about one mile in twenty minutes on an easy downhill pitch, you can apply this knowledge to travel down a river canyon. You will know after an hour of walking that your party has gone about three miles, or slightly less if you have taken rest stops. An experienced backpacker using this crude form of dead reckoning can calculate his progress quite accurately.

A *hat* can also be a useful item on a backpacking trip. Many persons need a hat to shield their heads and necks from the sun. This is especially true for older men. The traditional solution to this problem is a crushable-type, felt, brimmed hat. The brim must be crushable, or else the frame of your backpack will "work" against it. These hats have a brim that bends down out of the way of your packframe.

Another solution to the sunburn problem is provided by the use of a baseball hat and a light colored handkerchief around the neck. A *light-colored handkerchief* is used so that the sun's heat will be reflected instead of absorbed. An undershirt can perform this same function.

If you are the kind of person who gets a cold head at night, the best choice of headgear is a Navy *watchcap* or a *wool ski cap.* Navy watchcaps can usually be bought in surplus stores for a dollar or two and are well worth it. They will not only keep your head warm, but can be pulled down over your ears to keep them warm, too.

A *pair of gloves* can be a real blessing on a cold autumn trip. Often it is inconvenient or impossible to put your hands in your jacket pockets when wearing a backpack. Consequently, cold hands can be a real nuisance on cold days. This is more frequently a problem with women, whose small hands cool more quickly than men's. Men should consider the little lady's gloves an investment in her good temper on falltime trips. In the summer season, gloves are generally not needed unless altitudes above the tree line are to be encountered.

Long underwear, like gloves, should be carried only when cold conditions are expected. If such conditions are expected, do not hesitate to take long underwear along. Cold winds can blow hard in the high mountains, especially above the tree line, and a pair of jeans does not afford adequate protection.

Long underwear can also be helpful if your sleeping bag is inadequate for the temperature conditions that you expect. For instance, if freezing temperatures are anticipated, but you have a down bag with only two pounds of fill, a suit of long underwear might provide an adequate margin of warmth.

The following items represent more frivolous accessories, which some backpackers look upon as necessities. Good advice is to improvise as suggested, unless you simply could not tolerate the absence of the stated item. If you start taking things like these, watch the weight of your backpack go out of sight!

Backpack Rain Cover — Represents our first step into the world of back-packing trivia. While a waterproof rain cover is a handy thing to have, especial-ly when it rains, it can be substituted for by the use of (1) a groundcloth tied on with a length of cord or (2) a large plastic trash bag tied on similarly.

Sleeping Bag Liner — This item is for those who do not want to get the insides of their sleeping bags dirty. They can also be useful when temperatures too cold for the bag's rating are expected. Such liners add a little warmth. You would be safer if you brought along a suit of long underwear in case the liner does not fulfill its promise.

Air Pillow — If your head simply must rest on a plastic pillow at night, this is just the item for you. Most people just roll up their jackets or other clothes and put them under their heads at night.

Eggers — Provide a great way of carrying eggs without worrying about break-age; but after you have used the eggs, what do you do with it? You guessed it: you are left with another useless item to carry. A solution to the empty-egger-carrying-problem is to pack eggs in a small cardboard box, being careful to cushion them with newspaper, styrofoam, or another burnable material. Pack-ing eggs this way lets you get rid of the container when you get rid of the eggs. To some people, just the thought of broken eggs would cancel out this item.

Hatchets — These are totally unnecessary in the wilderness. If you need to cut wood, either break it with your foot or leave it. Generally, if you cannot break a piece of wood with your foot it is too green to burn. Logs can be "fed" into your campfire. Cutting green wood is illegal in National Parks.

Radios — These are generally frowned upon by backpackers, and for good reason. Weight and bulk do not provide insurmountable barriers to taking a radio along, but other considerations should be taken into account—primarily aesthetics. Radios in the wilderness can be compared with billboards on high-ways in that they both obstruct the view. Billboards obstruct the visual image; radios obstruct the sensory image. One can better enjoy nature without the rude interference of civilization in the form of a radio. Unless weather informa-tion is necessary, leave radios at home.

At this point, the reader is probably still baffled as to exactly how much his backpack will weigh. To help you estimate the loads that you will probably be carrying, I have compiled the list on the next page. Weights will naturally vary according to several factors.

First, how much comfort do you demand? If you carry fewer luxury items your pack will obviously be lighter.

Second, the weight of your equipment will make a difference. Specially designed lightweight backpacking equipment usually weighs less than the old Army equipment dug out of the basement.

And, third, the duration of the trip will affect the weight of your pack, mostly the result of carrying more or less food.

The list is based on the needs of two backpackers seeking moderate comfort on a five-day trip. Communal equipment is that equipment which is divided up between the parties. In the case of husband and wife teams, the woman will naturally carry a smaller share of this equipment. In all-man or "women only" parties, conflict is best avoided by apportioning this equipment equally.

INDIVIDUAL EQUIPMENT

Item	Weight (ounces)
Backpack (3 lbs.)	48
Sleeping bag with	
ensolite pad (5 lbs.)	80
Jacket or parka (2 lbs.)	32
Extra change of underwear	6
Two extra pairs of socks	5
Pair of shorts	5
Poncho or raincoat (plastic)	12
Personal toiletries	12
Knife	4
Sunglasses and case	3
Matchcase or bookmatches	2
Canteen (1 quart) plastic	3
Ski cap or felt hat	3
Fork and spoon	2
Pocketbook	8
Small towel	3
Supply of facial tissue	4
Wallet or miscellaneous item	5
Insect repellent	3
Total	(15 pounds) 240

COMMON EQUIPMENT

Item	Weight	
Cookware	2 lbs.	0 ozs.
Tube Tent (2-man)	2	0
Cord for above	0	3
First Aid kit	1	5
Maps & compass	0	5
Flashlight	0	3
Food for 5 days (computed at 1½ lbs. per day times 2 persons)	15	0
Total	21	0

Each person carries half of 21 lbs., or about 10½ pounds.

OPTIONAL COMMON EQUIPMENT

Item	Weight	
Camera with film	1 lb.	0 oz.
Stove and fuel	2	8
Total	3	8

Each person carries half, or 1 lb. 12 oz.

OPTIONAL PERSONAL EQUIPMENT

Fishing equipment	1 lb. 2 oz.

TOTAL LOAD FOR EACH PERSON

Individual equipment	15 lbs.	0 oz.
Common equipment	10	8
Optional common equpt.	1	12
Optional personal equpt.	1	12
Total	29 lbs.	0 oz.

As can be readily seen by the above total, careful consideration must be given in deciding whether or not to assume the burden of non-essential items such as stoves, cameras, tents, and extra clothes. This is especially true in the case of men traveling with women. As stated before, women are generally uncomfortable carrying more than twenty pounds. If this recommended load is not to be exceeded, the male partner can expect to carry three-quarters of the common equipment and all of the optional equipment. One can easily see the weight of the male partner's pack soaring over the forty pound mark if extreme restraint is not used in packing "extras."

CHAPTER 4

FOOD

Eating good food on the trail is very important above and beyond its nutritional value. The psychological component is equally important. A tasty and filling meal puts one in a better frame of mind. You become more relaxed and at ease. An ill-fed backpacker is more likely to become irritable and quarrelsome. It is suggested that menus be carefully planned according to group preferences. They should not be left to one person. If one person does not like rice, do not plan meals which rely heavily on rice. Individual tastes should not be forced upon a group. Try to take everyone's tastes into consideration. Such planning reinforces cohesiveness and averts dissension when out on the trail.

A hard day on the trail will consume about four to five thousand calories. Such a tremendous expenditure of energy builds mighty appetites. You might be able to skimp on food for a day or two, but not eating enough food will sap your energy and ruin an otherwise pleasant experience. Regardless of what else you take, carry adequate food for every meal. If you are dieting, do not try to do it on the trail. Even if you are eating well, you will probably lose weight. Dieting on the trail will starve your body of vitally needed vitamins, proteins and minerals.

What *should* you eat, then? Ideally, one's caloric intake would be satisfied by a heavy intake of fats. Fatty foods such as oils, bacon, cream, margarine and nuts contain about twice as many calories (by weight) as substances strong on carbohydrates such as rice, bread, cereals, crackers, fruits, and potatoes. Unfortunately, fatty foods have proven themselves to be poor in digestability at high altitudes and under trail conditions. Furthermore, fatty foods are generally more difficult to package and prepare, with the exception of nuts, than carbohydrate-rich foods. Thus, unless you are experienced in eating fatty foods on the trail, it is best to stick to carbohydrate-rich food for your main source of calories.

Naturally you should also eat plenty of protein foods like cheese, eggs, dried meats and fresh fish. Like fatty foods, protein foods are generally difficult to package, with the exception of cheese. They can only be carried fresh or dried. Because of spoilage, fresh protein like fresh eggs and cream cheese should generally be carried only a few days before eating. Dried protein, on the other hand, can be carried for long periods without spoiling, but tends to be expensive and lacks palatability. Despite the fact that proteins are either difficult to preserve or are lacking in taste, you should plan your menu so that it provides you with some protein at least once a day.

Eating a balanced diet is always necessary, but it is especially important when you are out on the trail. A backpacker's diet should be nutritious and easily digestible. Such a diet will usually be heavy on carbohydrates and proteins.

Food will usually be the heaviest and bulkiest item in your pack, so every attempt should be made to keep it both light and compact. Do not carry around a lot of cardboard and foil packaging. Try to avoid cans, and never take glass jars unless absolutely unavoidable. On long trips, you will find that you are severely limited on the size of things that you are carrying. So scrutinize the nutritional value of bulky items. For example, corn flakes might taste good, but their bulk makes them a poor choice for a breakfast cereal. The new Granola-type cereals offer a much better "bulk-to-nutrition" ratio than conventional breakfast cereals.

Finally, do not short-change yourself on food. Take enough food with you. You are going to want to eat a lot, and a well-fed backpacker is a happy backpacker.

Packaging

Your primary concern in packaging your food is to reduce the bulk. To this end you should attempt to get rid of as much packaging material as is feasible. While it is almost impossible to reduce the weight of your food substantially, it is quite easy to reduce its bulk.

The author has found that the best tools for this job are some used plastic bread bags, a package of plastic sandwich bags, a roll of cellophane tape, a few rubber bands, an indelible marker (Sanford's Sharpie is a good one) and a pair of scissors.

All powdered foods such as pancake mix, instant mashed potatoes, rice, sugar, dried milk, and bulk-packed powdered drinks etc. should be repacked in plastic sandwich bags and sealed. Quantities should be measured according to their anticipated use, and repacked accordingly. For instance, if you want a quart of milk for breakfast, measure the amount of powdered milk needed for a quart with a measuring cup. Dump the powder directly into a sandwich bag. Direct the powder to one corner of the bag, grab the excess part of the bag, and twist it until it comes tight with the powder. Carefully attach a piece of cellophane tape around the twist where it meets the powder, and cut off the excess part of the plastic bag with scissors, resulting in a somewhat heart-shaped bag. A number of these bags, organized by type of food or by type of meal, can then be packed into the used plastic bread bags. You can double-bag everything if you worry about holes or tears and subsequent spillage.

This may sound like a lot of trouble just to pack a few quarts of milk or beverage, but actually it isn't when you consider the benefits. First, the package is exceptionally compact and very lightweight. Second, by just biting or cutting off the lower end of the packet, you can empty the entire contents neatly into a canteen or other receptacle. Third, it provides you with just the quantity you need without having to fumble with measuring when you are hungry. Fourth, the package is not easily crushed or punctured. And last, it is ecologically sound. It can be completely disposed of in the evening campfire. It leaves no waste residue to spoil a beautiful campsite.

Many people like to take condiments along such as jellies, preserves, mustard or catsup. Rather than taking a heavy and breakable glass jar along, such substances are better packed in leakproof plastic jars or tubes. Several camping supply dealers market such jars and reusable washable plastic tubes. The tubes, which look like toothpaste tubes, are made of pliable plastic and are sealed at the end by means of a plastic sleeve which prevents the contents from escaping.

An effort should also be made to get rid of cardboard packaging. The only exception to this would be cardboard cracker packages, which would leave you with a bag of crumbs if eliminated. Cardboard boxes increase the bulk of your load tremendously. Throw away all boxes if possible. If the inner container is paper, as with gelatin desserts, repackage in plastic. The paper inner bag alone will almost certainly rupture in your packbag, and will make an incredible mess. Dried foods are frequently double-packaged in cardboard boxes. Get rid of the outer packaging. Carrying that extra cardboard around defeats the whole purpose of buying dehydrated food in the first place.

Of course, for weekend jaunts such complete repackaging is not necessary. Nevertheless, even on short trips weight can mount up very quickly. If one is not ounce careful, he will wind up being pound foolish.

What Foods to Take

If you do not know what to take, stick with the things that you eat at home. Always keep an eye on weight and bulk, though. It is amazing to find out that many of the things that you eat at home are suitable for backpacking. Examples include rice, dried soups, spaghetti, tea, pancakes, and countless other things.

Many persons who go backpacking carry nothing but dehydrated foods manufactured especially for backpacking. This is fine, and such people will probably be carrying loads that are somewhat lighter than campers relying more on regular store-bought foods.

On the other hand, dehydrated foods have certain disadvantages which one should consider before stocking up on them.

Dehydrated specialty foods are very costly. As a rule, they cost at least twice as much (on an ounce-for-ounce basis when reconstituted) as comparable foods which you can purchase in a supermarket.

Weight savings are not always that considerable, and in some cases are nonexistent, as in the case of powdered drinks and pancake mixes.

Often the prepackaged main course that "serves four" is inadequate for four persons with hearty appetites. Consequently, the main course must be supplemented by other foods. This will obviously increase the overall weight of the meal. It is always a good idea to prepare these foods at home before taking them backpacking. This will assure you of palatability and sufficient quantity.

Last, dehydrated foods, especially the "main course" dinners, are often made with inferior quality food products. Starch is a common ingredient, which is high in carbohydrates but low in other nutritional qualities. Another example is the use of beef-flavored soy flour in place of real freeze-dried beef. Often the use of preservatives and flavorings takes precedence over the nutritional quality of the item. And sometimes the product is not only nutritionally inferior, but it doesn't even taste good. In some cases these flavorings and preservatives leave an "aftertaste" in your mouth.

These things are pointed out, not so much to deter the reader from using dehydrated foods, but to look upon them with a critical eye. More often than not you can whip together a very tasty meal that will be of comparable weight to a dehydrated meal; it will taste as good; and it will cost half as much. Dehydrated specialty foods comprise less than twenty-five percent of an experienced backpacker's food stores. Admitted, some dehydrated foods provide a welcome change to an otherwise boring diet. After all, how else could you have scrambled eggs or strawberries after a week on the trail?

Nevertheless, most foods that you will need can be purchased in your local supermarket. Here is a list of some typical foods that can be purchased in a supermarket and handily used on a backpacking trip:

Rice — is probably the most nourishing food that you can take backpacking. Converted or quick rice cooks up quickly and is an excellent alternative to potatoes. It is, however, less nutritious and bulkier than regular unconverted long grain rice. Converted rice takes about fifteen minutes to cook, while unconverted rice takes thirty minutes or more. Rice is a good "base" for stews and soups. Even the more nutritional brown rice can now be purchased as a quick-cook rice.

Mashed potato flakes — are an excellent source of carbohydrates and, like rice, are a good filler-up food. Potato flakes can also be used for thickening stews.

Spaghetti — is an excellent source of carbohydrates. It fits all the requirements for backpacking by being concentrated and highly nutritious. Spaghetti can be added to soups as noodles or can be eaten with sauce as a main dish. Always buy thin spaghetti, as it cooks faster. (Thin spaghetti can now be bought that is made from more nutritive flours such as whole wheat, vegetables, soy, etc.)

Oatmeal — is a good breakfast food. It is light, compact and very nutritious. One of its advantages is that it cooks fast and really warms you up on a cold morning.

Pancake mix — is a must on backpacking trips. If you look hard on your grocer's shelves, you will eventually find a mix that does not require you to add fresh eggs. Such mixes require that you only add water for your batter, and the results generally are not bad. If you like your trout "floured" before frying, dip them in pancake mix instead of plain flour. The taste is really outstanding. Pack the mix in plastic bags as with other powdery foods. You can add wheat germ to your mix to make it more nutritional. Finally a reminder. Do not add the mix to the water. Add the water to the mix a little at a time; otherwise you might be stuck with a soupy mess.

Biscuit mixes — are popular among some backpackers as a change of fare after breadless days on the trail. These mixes can easily be "baked" in a "Boy Scout  oven," consisting of the pan and plate of a Boy Scout mess kit. Be sure that you bring along eggs, or be sure that none are needed. Also, do not place the "oven" too close to the fire. Better that you should bake it slowly and take an hour than to burn it.

Crackers — while being bulky, are usually looked upon as being a necessity in most backpackers' diets. Everyone has his favorite; however, if you like saltines, take Waverly Wafers, as they have the highest weight-to-bulk ratio of any saltine.

Granola — is a highly nutritious trail food made of rolled oats, brown sugar, coconut, nuts, wheat germ and bran. It can be eaten as a cold breakfast cereal with milk, or just munched at on the trail. It is generally available in health food stores.

Macaroni and cheese mixes — come packed in complete, ready-to-fix packages which are great for breakfast or dinner. Unfortunately, these mixes tend to be too bulky for long trips.

Pemican — an excellent trail mix that is very high in nutritive value, con - sisting of a mixture of almonds, walnuts, raisins, prunes (dried), extra dry dates, shredded coconut, dried vegetables, and dried meat.

Seeds — are great for chewing or nibbling on the trail. Good trail-eating seeds include chia, pumpkin, and sunflower.

Dried fruits — are available in most grocery stores, but you may have to look hard. Most are already packed in plastic bags, so you can just shove them in your pack. Most inexpensive are apples, which come both sliced and diced. Sliced apples are good to eat on the trail at lunchtime, and diced apples make a very filling applesauce dessert when cooked over a fire after dinner. Always cook a lot so you will have some for breakfast too. Other dried fruits include peaches, apricots, pears, raisins, an extra-dry type of dates, and prunes (get them pitted). Raisins especially are one of the best trail foods available. They are tasty and rich in vitamins and iron.

Dried soups — are quickly prepared and provide a tasty appetizer. Most come packaged in a form that can be thrown directly into your packbag. Furthermore, they usually have the directions written on the envelope inside the box. Just throw the outer box away. Dried soups also provide a great base for "trailstews." Dried powdered mixed vegetables can also be purchased, by the pound, and used in soups, etc.

Dry milk — should be packed in plastic bags, as previously described. Several brands are presently marketed in paper-covered foil packets, but the author has found them to be inferior to plastic, as they can break open under normal backpacking conditions. Dry milk and cocoa mix make a great drink morning or night. It is preferable to buy a cocoa mix that is readily soluble in cold water.

Cheese — is a great energy food high in both calories and protein. Unfortunately, there are very few kinds of cheese which are usable for backpacking. This is due to the need for cheeses to be refrigerated. Kraft Velveeta is one popular brand used by backpackers quite successfully. Unprocessed cheese is usually safe to carry for a day without fear of its spoiling. Some canned cheeses can be carried indefinitely, but be sure to read the label to confirm that this is the case.

Beef jerky — can be bought commercially or made at home. It is an excellent treat for lunch or just eating on the trail. It provides a chewy addition and adds necessary salt to the diet.

Spicy beef sticks — for lunches or snacks, a good source of protein and salt.

Canned meats — should be considered as an alternative to freeze-dried meats. If prudence is used, the weights should not be considered prohibitive.

Canned boned chicken — is a tasty addition to the campfire menu. It can be fixed in stews, or eaten plain with quick-cooking gravy brought in a separate package.

Canned bacon — can be considered for consumption on short trips, or even eaten the second morning out on longer trips. Canned bacon is just as good as regular refrigerated bacon, and tastes even better outdoors. Some campers prefer beef bacon, which keeps better than pork bacon.

Canned chipped beef — is often used to make a trail version of creamed chipped beef.

Corned beef — is packed in handy tins which will easily feed two persons. Just heat and serve.

Canned shrimp — provides an excellent base for shrimp creole or with Spanish rice and also adds necessary salt to your diet.

Tuna fish — is high in protein and calories. It makes any vegetable stew taste great. It is also good when eaten plain on crackers.

Salami — especially Italian dry salami, is a great lunch snack on the trail. It will keep well, but should be wrapped carefully to prevent the fat from getting all over, and to at least partly hide the smell from any hungry bears. Many persons find salami difficult to digest at high altitudes, so do not take it unless you have a cast-iron stomach.

Peanut butter — is a good lunch food, but like salami can be difficult to digest because of the high fat content.

Chocolate — is an absolute necessity on any backpacking trip. Most backpackers prefer the big bars of chocolate rather than smaller individual bars. Big bars take up less room. Regular chocolate will almost always melt during the day but will resolidify at night with minimal loss of taste. Semi-sweet chocolate does not melt as easily and is preferred by some. Hershey makes a tropical chocolate for those who expect to encounter extreme temperatures, but it tends to be far more expensive than regular chocolate. Wrap each bar in a plastic bag.

Tea and coffee — are good on any trip. Instant coffee is often sold in foil packets which contain just enough for one cup.

Bouillon cubes — provide a good warmer-up drink before dinner or at lunch. They are cheap, light, and taste good. They also provide a welcome change of drink.

Sugar — for drinks should be double wrapped to prevent a mess in case of a leak. Use rubber bands as closures instead of wire twists, which could puncture the bag.

Brown sugar (or raw sugar) — Just mix brown sugar in boiling water using two to three parts brown sugar to one part water. Serve hot on flapjacks.

Jams and jellies — are great on crackers or pancakes, but are quite heavy. A good idea is to leave them at home on long trips. Carry jams and jellies only in leakproof plastic jars.

Instant beverages — are tasty and refreshing on the trail. The best beverages are those which contain sugar, as they provide needed energy. My favorite is Wyler's, which manufactures several different flavors. The drinks are heavy (3 oz.), but are well worth the weight. Some hikers prefer the saccharin-sweetened drinks. These drinks, of course, provide no caloric nourishment. They also tend to leave an "after-taste" in your mouth. Do not skimp on instant drinks. Plan to use about one per day per person.

Gelatin mixes — are always carried by veteran backpackers. Hot gelatin mix is a great heater-upper at the evening campfire. Just dissolve the powder in boiling water and drink. It is rich in protein besides being a good hot drink. When packing, throw away the box and put the inner sack in a plastic sandwich bag.

Salt — can be purchased in convenient picnic-style throw-away containers at any grocery store. Be sure to carry an adequate supply. Some campers prefer individual salt packets, which usually must be purchased at a camping specialty store. If you prefer to buy your salt this way, be sure that the packets are water resistant plastic and not paper.

Shortening — in some form is a necessity on any mountain trip. Some backpackers prefer oleomargarine; others prefer a liquid oil. Liquid oils have an advantage in that they generally have a higher burning temperature. This can be important, especially if one is cooking on an open fire where temperatures can suddenly get very high. Most department stores carry plastic bottles into which you can put cooking oil and carry it without fear of its leaking. Still, be double safe and place the bottle inside a plastic bag. Allow for the use of one-half ounce per person per day. If you prefer to use oleomargarine, be very careful to purchase a brand which does not require refrigeration. It will usually say so on the label if it does require this. Such pure oleomargarines are usually the cheapest brands. They can be kept without refrigeration for many days. As with any potentially messy substance, pack carefully in a plastic bag.

Popcorn — is one of the best treats for backpackers. You will probably wind up eating more than you expected, so take plenty along. Cook it in your deepest covered pot. Heat the oil well before putting in the corn. Shake the pot as it pops and take it off the fire quickly when it stops popping, or you will have a burnt pot. Use plenty of salt.

Dried Foods

Below are listed some types of dried foods that might be taken on a backpacking trip. No special guidance is suggested here, as the extreme lightness of dried foods—and especially freeze dried foods—permits your palate to be your guide.

Taste quality varies from manufacturer to manufacturer, but as a rule, fruits and vegetables have excellent flavor. Meats are somewhat poorer in texture and flavor than the fresh product.

These items are generally purchased in mountaineering and sport shops. They are not usually available in grocery stores.

Freeze dried fruits — include apricots, apples, peaches and strawberries. These freeze dried fruits are excellent in flavor and texture. They can either be prepared in the conventional "add water" form or just popped into your mouth on the trail. If eaten in the latter way, just allow the fruit to "melt in your mouth" instead of chewing.

Extra dry dates — are very good and have much energy because of natural sugar they contain. Obtain from Covalda Dates, P.O. Box 908, Coachella, Calif. 92286 or from a health food store.

Dried vegetables—include string beans, kernel corn, peas, mushrooms, onions, cabbage, carrots, diced potatoes, and tomatoes. Some of these vegetables are freeze dried and others are vacuum dried—the difference being that freeze dried foods are quick frozen before the vacuum drying process is carried out. Thus this process does an excellent job of preserving the flavor and texture of the food.

In the case of vegetables, whether a product is freeze dried or just vacuum dried can make a great deal of difference or make no difference whatsoever. As tastes vary from person to person, this is a matter of individual discretion.

Most freeze dried vegetables are pre-cooked and require only the addition of water. As a rule, most vacuum dried vegetables need cooking. On the other hand, freeze dried vegetables cost, on the average, two to four times as much as vacuum dried vegetables.

Freeze dried meats — are often outrageously priced, but on long trips can provide a welcome change of fare. Included in this category are freeze dried pork chops, hamburgers, Swiss steak, ham, and meat balls. In the opinion of one who has tried these delicacies, the flavor and texture do not achieve the palatability of the "Real McCoy." If you choose to use any of them, make a sauce to pour over them or mix them in a stew.

Dried eggs — will probably never duplicate the taste of fresh eggs. The flavor can be helped somewhat by soaking the powder and water mixture overnight. Be careful not to overcook. Generally, dried eggs cannot be cooked "dry." When the cooked eggs start to weep, remove the heat, as the water will curdle out if cooked any longer.

Meat and bacon bars — are concentrated pre-cooked bars of pure meat. They are very tasty and are gaining popularity over freeze dried meats. They are great in stews or with just about anything. They are probably the best way to get rid of your craving for meat on the trail.

Dried main courses — are merely mixtures of the above mentioned dried foods usually with the addition of noodles and ersatz food products which have little if any nutritive value. You can eat better quality and probably better tasting meals if you mix the items yourself. Furthermore, by mixing your own stews you don't have to eat the carrots if you do not like them. You can just leave them out.

Pre-cooked freeze dried main courses — have recently appeared on the grocers' shelves. They require only the addition of boiling water. The taste is satisfactory. They are bulky but light. Try them first before you lay in a supply for a backpacking trip.

Cooking and Eating

Everything pertaining to cooking on a backpacking trip must be concerned with lightness. This includes not only the foods you eat, but the utensils that you use to cook them with. It is foolish to spend countless dollars on freeze dried foods in order to skimp a few ounces, and then to take off on the trail with an iron skillet. This may sound like an absurd example, but not so. A young Rocky Mountain backpacker, whose pack contained only dried foods, informed me that he "never went out without an iron skillet." He then proceeded to praise the even heating characteristics of this piece of cookware. Now admittedly, the even-cooking characteristics of an iron skillet have improved many a meal, and use thereof is undoubtedly the "secret" of many a famous chef. Nevertheless, only the most obstinate person would argue that the virtues of an iron skillet offset its liabilities on a backpacking trip.

I cite this example only to demonstrate the restraint that one must exercise in packing cooking gear. Cooking gear can be heavy or light, bulky or compact. The decision is yours. It is possible for an individual to survive quite easily on a long trip with only an aluminum pot, a cup and a spoon. While most persons would prefer a few more utensils, it is hardly necessary to bring along half of your kitchen.

A smart backpacker is resourceful. He makes one item serve several functions. For instance, instead of taking along a teaspoon to eat with and a stirring spoon to cook with, he will bring along only a soup spoon to serve both purposes. Instead of bringing along plates to eat his evening stew out of, he will eat it out of his pan, or even right out of the pot. For the sake of expediency and the preservation of your "poor aching back," it is permissible to cheat a little on Emily Post in the wilderness.

Of course, the exact items that you bring will be your decision, but try to play your list of utensils with an eye to bulk and weight. The cook kits of most backpackers consist of variations on the following themes.

The most famous of all cooking outfits is the old Boy Scout mess kit. This consists of a cup, a small pot, a plate, and a frying pan, all of which nest into one unit. It is a very utilitarian outfit for small groups and need only be supplemented by a large "stew pot."

Another outfit that is very popular consists of a larger nesting-style unit which contains two pots, one with a lid which converts into a fry pan, and a windscreen device which is specially fitted to accommodate a liquid fueled stove. All of these items including the stove are fitted to nest into this remarkably small unit. Only fuel, cups, and silverware must be carried separately. This same unit has also been produced with Teflon® coating on the cooking surfaces.

Another popular outfit for more spartan backpackers consists of a fry pan, a Sierra Club cup, and a can opener. All boiling is done in "ten tins." These are No. 10 cans whose lids have been removed. Two holes are punched in the sides and a wire run through the holes. The result is an excellent deep pot which weighs very little. The bulk problem is solved by carrying the tin outside your pack.

More sophisticated and affluent back-packers should not scoff at No. 10 tins. They are an excellent piece of cookware for those who prefer to cook over an open fire. The deep pot can hold huge quantities of food and rarely boils over. The can is extremely lightweight and, best of all, can be thrown away at the end of the trip.

Ten Tin

Just as important as the weight and bulk of your utensils is what you cook in them. Make your meals easy to cook, and fast. Breakfasts should be quick-cooking unless you intend to spend the whole morning cooking and cleaning up. Dinners should also be easy to prepare. When you get off the trail in the afternoon, you'll be H*U*N*G*R*Y and will not want to wait long to eat. Dinner should take no longer than forty-five minutes to cook. This means that no single item will require more than thirty minutes of boiling. Keep in mind that the cooking times that manufacturers recommend must be extended at high altitudes.

Experienced backpackers prefer to cook stews for dinner, because they are easy to cook, quick, and require but one large pot. Dinners should always be planned with an eye to convenience. Do not bring along a meal which requires several different pots each of which requires a different cooking time. Keep it simple. At the end of a long day just about anything tastes good. You will probably be too tired to play gourmet chef with four different pots, and certainly nobody will want to clean them.

The same holds true for breakfast. Keep cooking time to a minimum and nourishment at a maximum.

Why stress a breakfast with a minimal amount of cooking? Because at *best* it will probably take 1½ hours from the time you get up to the time you depart for your next day's trek. An extra ½ hour in camp represents over one mile of cool, comfortable morning hiking. Do not waste time; break camp quickly. This is not to say that the morning need be a big rush. A backpacking trip should be a relaxing vacation. But time spent tarrying over a morning fire is wasted time that would be more enjoyably spent on hiking breaks, or at lunchtime when you can relax in the warm sun.

As a rule, backpackers plan an uncooked lunch. This eliminates the need to wash dishes. Eating a cold lunch is not a hard and fast rule, but usually the noontime temperatures encountered in the mountains will be moderate enough that warm foods will not be necessary.

The following recipes have been tried by myself and others on backpacking trips. They are all reasonably lightweight, and rely mostly on foods readily available in grocery stores.

Breakfasts

"Tang" (cold)
tea with sugar
oatmeal with raisins

"Tang" (cold)
pancakes with brown
or raw sugar syrup

coffee with dry milk
and sugar
pancakes
applesauce (cold—
cooked the night
before

Oatmeal with brown
sugar
cooked dried apricots
coffee with dry milk
and sugar

Granola and milk
dried prunes
hot chocolate (milk
and cocoa mix)

Dried eggs mixed
with ½ bacon bar
hot tea with sugar

Potato pancakes
(Manischevitz)
hot applesauce
tea with sugar
(This meal takes a
long time to cook.)

"Tang"
Granola and milk
cooked dry peaches

Dinners (for two)

1 package macaroni & cheese
1 can tuna fish
lemonade mix
4 oz. sliced vacuum-dried peaches

1. Cook macaroni and cheese as directed; add tuna; reheat for a few minutes; serve.
2. Peaches require no cooking.
3. Mix lemonade as directed.

½ lb. spaghetti
1 can (6 oz.) tomato paste
1 envelope spaghetti sauce mix
lemonade mix

If using single-burner stove:
1. Cook spaghetti sauce as directed.
2. Cook spaghetti and drain.
3. Reheat sauce if necessary
4. Mix lemonade as directed.

1 packet dry soup or bouillon
1 packet potato flakes
1 can evaporated milk
1 packet chicken gravy mix
1 can boned chicken

1. Cook soup and eat separately.
2. Prepare mashed potatoes as directed.
3. Cook up gravy and add chicken.

1 packet dry soup or bouillon
1 envelope Spanish rice mix
1 cup quick cooking rice
1 can shrimp
1 packet gelatin

1. Cook soup and eat separately.
2. Boil Spanish rice mix a few minutes. Add quick cooking rice and shrimp. Cook 5 minutes more.
3. Cook up hot flavored gelatin mix for dessert.

4 oz. cooked dried apples
1 package macaroni & cheese
4 oz. sliced salami

popcorn

1. Cook apples for about ½ hour.
2. Cook macaroni & cheese as directed—eat with salami.
3. Cook popcorn in deep pot; cover bottom of pot with oil; heat; add popcorn and pop.

Note: Many backpackers do not realize that eating burnt food or drinking burnt cocoa or chocolate can cause serious stomach upsets, which is another good reason care should be taken in the performance of cooking tasks.

Teddi

CHAPTER 5

STOVES AND FIRES

One of the biggest controversies among backpackers is whether to use a stove or cook over an open fire. The stove has several advantages. It gives off even heat. It is always available for immediate cooking, and it does not cover your pots and pans with soot. The liability in carrying a stove along is, of course, its weight and bulk.

Purists who extol the spartan tradition of America's early mountaineers will naturally condemn the use of stoves in the wilderness. (If men were meant to use stoves in the wilderness, God would have placed them there, they say!) Such purists will sing the praises of the evening cooking fire and extol the joys of natural mountain living. Such logic, however, is of another era. If everyone adhered to such an ethic, there would be no modern-style backpacks, and we would still be slipping and sliding down the trail with leather soles on hiking boots.

In a more contemporary sense, stoves have indeed earned a place in wilderness backpacking. Modern backpacking stoves are both light enough and compact enough to be carried into the wilds. Furthermore, they have an ecological importance. In campsites along heavily used trails and in many national recreational area campgrounds, the forest floors have been picked virtually clean of deadwood. The decomposition of this deadwood, especially in western areas where there is little dropping of leaves in the fall, provides the forest's major source of soil nutrients. Furthermore, the worms and termites in this dead wood provide a source of food for birds such as woodpeckers. While it is difficult to predict the ultimate effect of wood-gathering, it is probably safe to say that it is detrimental to the forest's ecology. It would be imprudent to say that this is not the case, when one considers that we will probably not be around in three hundred years to see the effect of such wholesale wood gathering.

Taking a broad ecological perspective, then, stoves have a definite place in the wilderness. Using stoves reduces deadwood comsumption in heavily used areas and could possibly minimize the effect of man's presence in such areas.

I am in no sense passing judgment against evening campfires. This is a mountain tradition that is almost sacrosanct. But even the most stolid defenders of the spartan tradition must admit that by eliminating the use of wood for cooking, deadwood consumption can be halved.

In certain circumstances, the question of whether or not to use a stove might prove to be purely academic. In many wilderness areas the overuse of existing firewood has forced the authorities to make the use of cooking stoves mandatory. In such areas campfires of any type are prohibited.

In certain other cases, nature dictates the use of a stove. Carrying a stove above the tree line is highly advisable, and is usually a necessity. I also found it a good idea to carry one on the trails in the Pacific Northwest where rain-soaked deadwood neither dries quickly nor lights easily.

In circumstances other than this, a stove will usually be seen as a useful addition to your pack. Stoves are light, clean, convenient, and ecologically virtuous. With a little training, even a ten-year-old can safely operate a modern lightweight camp stove.

Only a few things need be remembered. First, do not waste fuel. Turn the stove off when you finish cooking. Second, turn the heat down when the pot begins to boil vigorously. Once a dish is boiling vigorously, it will not increase in temperature. Keeping the heat up only wastes fuel. The dish will not cook any faster.

Third, carry fuel in a good-quality metal container. Plastic containers should never be used for fuel storage. Also, test the container for leakage before the trip.

Finally, be sure that the fuel you use is absolutely free of impurities. If in doubt, filter it yourself.

Whether you take a stove with you or not, the chances are that you will have some kind of campfire most nights on the trail. Not knowing how to build a campfire defeats or frustrates many campers who are inexperienced. Lacking large quantities of newspaper and start-er fluid, a wilderness camper must know how and where to start a fire.

Most important is, of course, where to put the fire. In nine out of ten cases, this decision will already have been made for you. In other words, the campsite that you choose will already have a fire pit. If there is one, use it. Do not build another fire pit. Doing so will detract greatly from the pristine beauty of a campsite. Extra fire pits mean more ashes around a campsite; they mean more fire-blackened rocks, and they mean a messier campsite for the next occupant. Build second fire pits only as a last resort.

If you must build another fire pit, or improve on an already exist-ing one, follow these rules. Choose an area that is well clear of low-lying limbs, especially dead ones. Placing a campfire under a tree is an invita-tion to disaster. Clear the area around the fire of twigs and pine needles for a distance of at least eight to ten feet. And, finally, line the edges with good-sized rocks.

Now then, how do you start a fire? If one observes the following directions carefully, he will become a fire builder "par excellence."

First, you must remember that a fire requires three things—heat, air and fuel. If you lack any of these components, it will be impossible to start or maintain a fire. In *starting* a campfire, air and fuel are of most critical importance. If one arranges his fuel properly so that it is adequately ventilated, only the small amount of heat supplied by a match is needed to start a roaring fire.

To start the fire you must use the very smallest twigs or dead pine needles. Arrange them in an open box-like pile so that they are well ventilated, then light with a match. If the twigs do not burn, they are wet. Kindling must be dry. If it turns red but does not flame up, blow on the red kindling, gently. If it does not flame up, but slowly burns away, put more kindling on top. Put on only a little at a time so as not to smother the red kindling. Then blow again gently and evenly until it flames up. Before doing anything, continue to blow on the flames until they generate enough heat to burn without the fanning action of your breath. Then proceed to add progressively larger kindling to the fire; small branches first, then larger branches, but always arranged in a way to allow air to circulate in the fire pile. Put logs on the fire only when large branches burn easily in the flames and there is a bed of coals below.

If you are cooking over the fire, place rocks in the bed of the fire-place and build the fire around these rocks. When it is time to cook, you will have platforms upon which to place your pots.

Anyone who has ever cooked over an open fire knows that the outsides of pots become covered with soot which must be laboriously scrubbed off. A good way to minimize the difficulty in scrubbing pots is to put soap, plain soap, all over the outsides. Only a little is necessary. When you go to wash your hands, just rub soap off your hands onto the pots and pans. This can be done to the morning's cookware the night before. When cookware is thus "soaped" before cooking, the black film of soot will effortlessly wash away at clean-up time.

When cooking, watch the pots carefully and stir frequently. An open fire can be very hot. The food at the bottom of the pots can burn easily if not frequently stirred. Food can also boil over quickly. Keep a careful watch on it, and do not handle pots with your bare hands. One unthinking move can put your hand out of action for several days. Always keep your wits about you around fire. Handle pots with sticks or with a potholder.

In no circumstances should you leave a fire unattended. Fire is the greatest enemy of the wilderness. Do not take chances with it. It takes only one mistake in ten thousand incidents to destroy many square miles of wilderness. Thus, when through, soak the fire thoroughly with water until every coal is put out. Stir to make sure. If no water is available, bury the fire under dirt that consists mainly of crushed rock. Never bury a fire under humus-rich soil, or soil which is rich in decomposing vegetable matter. A fire buried under humus-rich soil can burn for *weeks* and could possibly spread to trees.

Shearer

Cleaning up After Meals

There is probably no activity on a backpacking trip that is less desirable than cleaning up the dishes after meals. Nevertheless, it must be done, so why not do it as painlessly as possible?

A first step along this path is deciding upon who is going to do the washing. Experience has shown me that much quarreling and disagreement can be avoided by deciding before the trip on a system of strict rotation of this chore. In other words, a different group member does the chore after each meal. Lunch is usually not included, as it is usually a cold meal requiring few washables. This system of rotation is best, because it provides no way for one person to weasel out of his job. When it's his turn, he has to do it.

Start cleaning up during the meal. Right after the main course is served up—usually out of the largest pot—fill the pot with water and put it right back on or next to the fire. Also place a small piece of soap or some soap shavings into the pot. While you are eating, it will heat up and loosen any burnt-on food at the bottom of the pot.

At the end of the meal, pour the soapy water into the other pans and dishes. Fill them all with the soapy water so that the food can loosen while you scour them with a soap pad or steel wool. When you are finished scouring, dump the water on the ground, NOT in the stream or river by which you are camped. Preferably dump it 50 to 100 feet away from any water source to prevent pollution. Most soap pads and detergents contain phosphate compounds which pollute the water and leave an ugly scum and bubbles in lakes and streams. Rinse the dishes in a similar manner, being careful to dump the waste on the ground away from the water source.

Even so-called "biodegradable" soaps leave residues in the streams, the only difference being that their component compounds are ultimately broken up by the action of bacteria and sunlight.

The only occasion when it might be tolerable to pollute in this manner is in washing your hands or body. In such case you should use only soap or a "biodegradable" detergent or organic cleaning compound.

One of the rules that a good woodsman follows is that of being considerate of the people who are using the same water supply as himself. To keep pollution at a minimum, follow the aforementioned pollution-minimizing guidelines.

Before leaving your camp, clean up thoroughly, leaving no litter. If possible, leave a camp cleaner than you found it. More and more of us

must set such good examples in order to counter that terrible polluter
of the wilderness, the litter bug.

CHAPTER 6

ON THE TRAIL

At last you are out on the trail. Behind are the food stores, the sport shops and the packing. Finally you are out on your own.

The usual impulse of the green backpacker is to put as many miles as he can between himself and the road head as quickly as possible. This is a mistake. Relax and take it easy. Enjoy the scenery. The imprudent backpacker who tries to set records on his first day out is looking for trouble.

Most backpackers, and especially adult backpackers hitting the trail for the first and possibly only time that year, are not in the best of condition physically. A week-long outing can be ruined if such a person tries to put ten to fourteen miles under foot the first day out. Even if such an extended outing has been preceded by a weekend outing and some physical training, endurance limits should not be tested. Testing such limits will result in sore backs, sore legs, stiff necks, and blistered feet.

Your first day on the trail should be a short one. Plan on a hike not to exceed eight miles. This plan will give you plenty of time to rest on the trail. It will also let you be sure of reaching camp before sundown even if you get a late start. If traveling in a group, such a plan will assure a minimum of chaos on the first day out.

You should always take it easy on the trail, but this is especially important on the first day. Set a leisurely pace. It is better to set a pace which increases your normal breathing rate moderately, but not to the point where you are panting for air. If you are hiking at such a rate, you should be able to carry on a running conversation on all but very steep uphill stretches. Maintaining such a breathing rate ensures that you will open up blood circulation to usually unused areas of your lungs without exhausting yourself. This is important, as it facilitates your body's adjustment to the lighter air at higher mountain altitudes. It also ensures that you will gain greater physical capability with each succeeding day in step with your expanding lung capacity. Try to maintain this breathing rate whatever the terrain upon which you are traveling. This means a slower pace on uphill stretches and a faster pace on downhill stretches. Never press your endurance on uphill stretches or passes. A steady plodding pace will get you to the top of a pass just as soon as and in better condition than a jackrabbit pace. Rhythmic hiking will put more miles under your feet in more comfort than any speed-demon method. Even when you do stop to rest or have a drink, you will be ready to resume walking more quickly because your body does not take as long to recover its equilibrium.

The fact that a low but steady level of exertion is more effective than a high level of exertion can be scientifically proven. It has long been known to those in the field of biological chemistry that lactic acid is one of the byproducts of the complex energy-producing process in the muscles. Lactic acid is the substance which makes muscles feel tired when we overexert them. When high levels of exertion are sustained, lactic acid builds up in the muscles. The results of this buildup are fatigue and sore muscles. Lactic acid can be removed only by "burning" it away with oxygen from our lungs. Thus, a speed-demon hiker must breathe harder and harder to keep the level of lactic acid in his muscles down. In mountain altitudes the air cannot supply a trail jackrabbit with enough oxygen to burn away his steadily increasing accumulation of lactic acid. Ultimately, gasping for breath, our speed demon must stop and rest until his body has burned away enough lactic acid for him to continue.

It is evident that the hiker who keeps a slower but steadier pace will have a smaller amount of lactic acid to rid himself of; thus his body will recover more quickly. The speed demon, on the other hand, will build up great quantities of lactic acid as a result of his strenuous spurts of exertion. This means longer stops for his body to obtain enough oxygen to burn away the lactic acid in his muscles.

Such bursts of exertion are also hard on one's muscle tissue, and provoke strains and sprains of muscles and tendons. Furthermore, the rest stops that a speed demon takes are not really rests, but just refueling stops. When such a person stops moving, the body's organs pound away in a rush to reestablish a normal equilibrium. Consequently, at day's end such a person will be more exhausted and tired than a back-packer who covered the same ground at a more reasonable pace.

Another way to get the most miles under your feet with a mini-mum of exertion is to get an early start in the morning.

In the mountains it is best to "live by the sun," that is, get up with the sunrise in the morning, and go to bed shortly after sunset. This rou-tine probably will conflict with your normal living schedule, but it serves a practical purpose—that is, getting you out on the trail when you can move most effectively.

The best hours for hiking are between eight and ten in the morning. At this time of day, the sun is still low in the sky, and the air is still cool from the night. As the sun climbs higher, the air becomes warmer and your body begins to function less efficiently.

Your body functions much like an automobile engine. On hot days your car loses power, and overheats. Like an automobile, your body tends to overheat and lose power when the temperature rises. On a hot afternoon in the mountains you will find yourself "overheating" on dif-ficult sections of trail, and you will have to stop to cool off. Morning hiking, on the other hand, is easier, as the cool air lets your body func-tion at optimal efficiency.

The morning provides optimal conditions for running off the miles. Even a large group should be able to put four miles under their feet in these first two hours of the day's jaunt. The trick, of course, is to get up early enough to get moving by eight o'clock.

One more reason for getting up early is simply that it is a very beautiful time of day to be up and about. The early morning sunshine in the mountains brings the birds out to sing, and the deer come out to graze. The small animals come out of their burrows to warm themselves on the nearest log. The sunrise usually brings with it a clear sky and calm air. It is a placid time of day that should not be missed. A good time to rise is between 6:15 and 6:45, when the sky is light and the sun has not yet peeked below the upper limbs of the tree under which you are sleeping.

Starting the day early is a point of great conflict in some groups. I strongly urge getting up early if it is physically possible. An early start's advantages far outweigh its disadvantages. Its primary disadvan-tage is that you have to crawl out of your nice warm bag into the c-o-l-d morning air. Another drawback is that the surfaces of sleeping bags, ground cloths, and tents tend to become covered with moisture, from condensation during the night. The obvious impulse in the morning is to delay packing these items until the sun rises high enough over head that its rays dry out the gear. On many summer mornings, I have passed backpackers camped next to the trail just sitting and waiting until their gear dried out! Little do they realize that the miles they hike that day will be more difficult because of their decision to dally.

As for the problem of wet bedding, there are two easy systems for drying sleeping bags. The first is to tie the bag loosely around the outside of your backpack. This can easily be done with a length of nylon cord or twine. The second, and more frequently used, method is just to pack up the damp gear and then spread it out at lunchtime under the hot midday sun. At that hour these items will dry quickly and thoroughly.

While it is not always possible to judge when you will stop for lunch, at least try to pick a good spot. My favorite spots are in river canyons with smooth slabs of granite along the edge of the river. Such places give you water, clean ground to sit on, a place to stretch out, and a place to dry out last night's bedding. Do not rush lunch. Take at least an hour. Relax and enjoy yourself. Noon is one of the nicest times of day in the mountains. The water in the streams is cold, the rocks are warm, and the sun beams down from its high perch in the sky. What more could a person ask for?

The first thing that I do at lunchtime is take off my boots and wade into the water for a few minutes. The sensation of the cool water against your feet can only be described as pure pleasure. Then just sit back and eat and rest, and maybe even sleep. Do not allow yourself to be hurried by time. Do not rush to the next night's campsite. There is no schedule binding you in the mountains. The next night's camp is on your back, and there are few places in the mountainous back country of America's west where you cannot drop your gear for a night.

The only person who rushes to his next camp is a strange and irrational mountain creature called the Trail Runner. This strange creature is a spirited beast whose existence is centered around one aim. That aim is to put as many miles of trail under his feet every day as is physically possible. He is occasionally seen sitting exhausted on a trailside rock, but is more often seen hot footing it along the trails. His usual habitat extends along the major trails of the west, notably the Pacific Crest Trail of the northwest and the John Muir Trail of California. He looks like any other backpacker, but rarely utters anything, as he is usually breathing too hard. On those rare occasions when the Trail Runner is engaged in a conversation, he usually proceeds to babble about the miles he has reeled off, the difficulties he has encountered, and the obstacles that remain ahead of him. His cerebral cortex seems crammed full of statistics on miles traveled and vertical rises encountered, but little else. At the end of his journey, he has traveled the same trails as other travelers. He has slept in the same campsites as they, and he has swept his eyes over the same panoramic views as they. But in fact, he has seen nothing and traveled nowhere. The Trail Runner has done nothing more than prove his own physical abilities. He has not seen the flowers, or heard the birds sing. He has not listened to the wind howl or seen the sun set. In short, he has missed all that is nature.

The lesson to be learned here is that you should not rush through a backpacking trip. You should take your time to enjoy the delights of nature. A trip through the wilderness is like a glass of fine wine. One does not guzzle it down; one sips it slowly, and savors each sip. A rest stop or a lunch break should be more than a mere refueling stop. Take a look around you. Enjoy the flowers and plants and animals. A quick passage down the trail is unimportant to a real backpacker. A real backpacker wants to travel down a trail *in order to enjoy nature* and learn something about the world around him.

A well planned trip will not cover more miles in a day than everyone in the group can comfortably handle. To some persons three miles is comfortable. Some persons can easily hike fifteen miles in one day over mountain terrain. I find about ten miles a comfortable distance. Still, if you are hiking in a group, distances traveled must often be computed before the start of the trip, in order to coordinate planning and individual vacation schedules. When traveling on a precomputed schedule, most groups find that they fall into a hiking pattern of fastest first and slowest last. Often the slower member or members of the group will fall back from the main body. If you are the speed demon, help the slowpoke with part of his load, thus slowing your pace and assuring greater speed for the group. Everyone's body chemistry functions differently. Some persons can sustain a high level of exertion better than others. Also, mountain altitudes, weather, temperatures and a thousand other factors affect a person's physical performance. Suggest that the slower group member take a salt tablet, a drink, or a piece of candy. This might be all he needs to get a new burst of energy. Take a rest stop in the shade for a few minutes before moving on. If fatigue persists, then try to make camp as early as is reasonably possible.

If you are the slowpoke or laggard of the group, put out a little extra effort, but do not carry it to the point of being ill. Never hesitate to ask the others to wait for you. In no circumstances say, "Go ahead; I will catch up later." The temptation to say this can sometimes be very powerful, especially when other group members are prodding and complaining. Experienced mountain backpackers know that leaving a fatigued group member behind can be an invitation to distress and even disaster. Mountain trails, especially in seldom traveled back country areas where trails are less well defined, can have "false starts," unexplained forks, and animal trails which can lead one astray. Such pseudo-trails can be invisible to one person's eye and quite plain to another's. The possibilities for a fatigued person's being led off the main trail are quite high. Such a person is probably tired, hot, and lacking in visual perception. This sort of person is more than likely to exercise poor judgment when left to his own devices.

Many things can happen to an individual in the aforementioned circumstances. He can lose the trail and become lost. He can sit down for a rest, fall asleep, and not wake until darkness has descended and the trail is impossible to follow. He may become sick and be lacking in the proper medical aids. Or he may have an accident which could disable him.

While all of the above conditions are not likely, their possibility is great enough that chances should never be taken. It is a fact that people have become lost because certain persons in a group were too eager to reach their goal.

This rule of not leaving anyone behind is one of the cardinal rules of back-country travel. It is also applicable to the case of an injured hiker. A disabled hiker should never be left alone. The only case in which an injured person might have to be left alone is if there is only one person with the injured party and aid is not expected for days. In such a drastic case, adequate food, water, and shelter must be arranged before leaving the person. Also, mark the location carefully by trail blazes, stones, and on a map. A rescuer should carry with him only maps, food and water to facilitate quick travel. Most areas of the country have facilities for airplane or helicopter rescue into wilderness areas. Consequently, the rescuer need not carry provisions for a return trip.

Hopefully, the aforementioned situation will never be encountered, but it is very important to be prepared and knowledgeable about what must be done.

Anyone who has ever hiked has almost certainly encountered trail switchbacks. Switchbacks are trails built on steep slopes that zig-zag back and forth across the slope. By ascending the slope at a regular rate of incline, the hiker is enabled to maintain his pace. Switchbacks not only provide an easy way for hikers to ascend steep slopes, but they also deter erosion caused by overly steep trails.

One popular "trick" of some backpackers is to cut straight down the slope between switchbacks when descending from a higher point. While this undoubtedly saves the backpacker a few seconds in hiking time, it also does great damage to the trail. In cutting down the slope, the unthinking backpacker is also damaging plant life, loosening soil and causing rocks to roll downhill. The result of this "time-saving" ploy is that our careless individual has provided a sluiceway for water during the spring runoff. This water will erode the soil and rocks he loosened, and will wash them down onto the trail below, blocking or damaging it. Plantlife destroyed by switchback cutters is slow to reassert itself where it has been damaged or washed away. In a similar way, the damage done by such individuals tends not to repair itself. Other thoughtless hikers tend to see the first person's shortcut and they too see fit to use it. Thus the damage is multiplied. So don't use shortcuts on trails!

Mountain trails are built at great expense to assure the hiker maximum ease in his travels. Damaging trails by cutting switchbacks reduces the comfort of others using the trail, and it means that the government will have to spend that much more on trail maintenance. Switchbacks were built for a purpose; please do not try to improve on them by trail cutting.

When crossing ridges, passes, and plateaus above the tree line, one will very likely encounter mounds of rocks called cairns. These rock piles are used to mark the trail and should not be disassembled.

Often trails over very rocky ground are only faintly distinguishable from the surrounding terrain. When such trails receive little use, wintertime snows and ice can shift the rocks so that the trail is completely indistinguishable. The cairns then provide the only trail markers. Large cairns are rarely completely destroyed by winter snows. If you are hiking through such an area, do your part to maintain these trail markers. Add stones to damaged cairns, and build cairns where none are seen. However, you should build cairns only when you are absolutely sure that you are on the trail.

A few years ago, I was exploring around an abandoned mining area just east of Yosemite National Park when I came upon a series of cairns.

As it turned out, the cairns marked a long since abandoned trail which led high up a mountain to an abandoned silver mine. The trail was almost completely indistinguishable, and was not marked on a map. But because it was marked by an excellent series of cairns, I was able to follow it easily. Had I not found this trail, it would have been nearly impossible to find my way up the mountain, much less find the mine. Such an experience emphasizes the importance of maintaining cairns, especially on seldom used trails.

Also frequently encountered in the mountains are streams which must be crossed. Most large mountain streams have bridges across them, but it is not altogether unheard of to encounter a small river with no bridge. More often, though, one will come across a small stream which is too big to jump across but too small to wade across. In such a case, you will probably be obliged to cross the stream by jumping across rocks or balancing yourself on a log like a tightrope walker. The experienced backpacker, having crossed hundreds of such obstacles, will merely hop, skip or jump his way across, but this same obstacle will strike terror into the heart of a first-timer. If you fit into this latter category, here are some simple ways to save yourself from getting wet feet and egg on your face. First, *untie your hip band.* This should always be done when crossing a stream. Second, check the crossing. If you are crossing on rocks, chart your every step first. Third, move across the stream quickly. Do not stop to balance yourself on a rock in mid-stream or in the middle of a log bridge. Look at where you are going to put your foot next; do not look down at the water. Looking at the moving water can cause you to lose balance. Finally, regardless of whether you are crossing on a log or rocks, check the surface beforehand to see if it is wet. If so, take extra care when you step on it. A thoughtful hint: a short-legged backpacker much appreciates his considerate companions if they place their rocky bridges at closer strategic distances than normal.

Some backpackers find it a great help to carry a walking stick. A long walking staff can give one an "extra leg" when crossing streams. It can also be helpful when passing through briers, to push them away as you pass through. Some ingenious persons use such staffs as tent poles. If you think that you might like a walking stick, take one along. Then, even if you change your mind and decide that you do not need it, you can use it for firewood.

As your mountain day wears on, you will probably find that your pace has slowed somewhat. Your body will probably not function as efficiently in the heat of the afternoon. Consequently, your afternoon schedules should generally be less rigorous than morning ones. Check your maps at lunchtime and set a mark for the end of the day's trek. This mark should be a place where good campsites are likely to exist. Preference should be given to places marked as campsites on maps. However, almost any place where the presence of water is indicated is acceptable. Remember that in the later summer months streams dry up. If the presence of water at the proposed site is doubted, ask backpackers coming from that direction if they found water. Also ask approaching parties if good campsites exist at your proposed goal, or if better ones are found elsewhere. Most wilderness areas have been backpacked into for years. Consequently, most major stream crossings and lakes will have campsites already waiting for you.

A mountain campsite is merely a fairly level cleared area for sleeping bags, a fire pit, and possibly a few logs to sit on. Water should always be nearby, and the sleeping area should be dry and level. It should be level because sleeping bags, and especially nylon ones, have a tremendous inclination to slide downhill in the middle of the night.

The best campsites are not directly exposed to the wind. This can be especially important when camped out in passes, on plateaus and next to lakes. If possible, park your sleeping bags next to some rocks or scrub bushes which will take the brunt of the wind. If wind is a secondary concern, then it is best to place sleeping gear in a spot where it will receive the warming rays of the morning sun.

After the campsite is chosen, the next step is to make dinner. I prefer to start cooking dinner as soon as I get into camp. This gives me plenty of time to clean up after the meal, and go out exploring the area around the campsite.

I find this evening exploration to be one of the most interesting times of the day. Animals are often astir at this time. If you are camped near a meadow, it is not unusual to see deer feeding. Birds are always singing away, and the wind blows between the leaves of the trees. As the sun descends, you return to camp to start a fire.

After dark, in front of the fire, your whole world of sight shrinks to only a few feet; yet the feel of the wilderness does not leave. Most evening nights are cool and clear, and a snack of hot gelatin hits the spot to warm you up before bedtime. When you do go to bed, take your canteen with you. The cold, dry mountain air can dry your throat while you are asleep. If you should wake up, you will not have to crawl out to get a drink.

Sleep tight, for tomorrow will be another wonderful day in the mountains.

Hiking Where the Air Is Rare

Almost by definition, mountains lie at high altitudes. Unless you are an easterner, mountains mean that you will encounter elevations of over five thousand feet. The Rockies, the Cascades, and the Sierra all have peaks over fourteen thousand feet, and most hiking in these areas is done at elevations over four thousand feet.

As one ascends above this elevation, the air thins rapidly. In more precise terms, this means that there are fewer molecules of oxygen in a given volume. Because there is less of this life-sustaining gas, breathing becomes labored. In such circumstances care should be taken not to overexert oneself. Overexertion can lead to nausea, headaches, loss of appetite, and total exhaustion. While these symptoms are not really dangerous, they can make a mountain outing a relatively unpleasant experience. They are the symptoms of what is commonly called altitude sickness. In some cases, this illness is observed at elevations as low as five thousand feet. Often the victim can overcome the sickness in a day or two, but the best cure is to return to a lower elevation. Sometimes a descent of just two or three thousand feet will make all symptoms disappear.

A good rule of thumb in planning mountaineering trips is to ascend as gradually as possible over a number of days. This gives one's body time to acclimate itself to the change in elevation. As an example, it takes the average person about one week to fully acclimate his body to nine thousand feet. This in no sense means that one has to take a week to work himself up from sea level to nine thousand feet. It only means that it takes a week of living at this elevation in order to do the things one can do at sea level with approximately the same amount of effort. However, if one is in fairly good condition, one's body can easily accommodate a weekend outing at six to eight thousand feet.

Another factor to be reckoned with at high altitudes is the sun. The atmospheric umbrella that we live under at lower elevations protects us from most of the sun's ultraviolet rays. With elevation, our exposure to these rays increases as the concentration of oxygen decreases. Thus, at high elevations most people, especially those with pale complexions, are susceptible to sunburn. This is especially true above the "tree line," where the lack of vegetation leaves one exposed to the full intensity of the sun all day. Extreme caution must be taken on snowfields in the summer. Only three or four hours of exposure to the sun on a snowfield can burn one's skin to a crisp.

In the summer of 1965, a Swiss friend and I spent a day ski touring on the Plateau Rosa snowfields above Zermatt, Switzerland. It was a delightful July day with the sun shining bright and clear. At the day's end we sat chatting on a rock above the teleferique which would take us back down to our hotel in Zermatt. It was only three o'clock, but I could already feel the heat coming off my face. By the next morning my face was bloated and swollen. It took a week for it to return to normal. This was a sad lesson indeed, and I for one will never again be caught without sun protection on summer snowfields or at high altitudes.

What then are the best sun protection products available? For medium to high altitudes (5,000-10,000 ft.) I would say that any of the well known commercial products is adequate. Such preparations are especially good if they contain a chemical which screens out ultraviolet rays. If you are feeling poverty stricken, a homemade lotion can be prepared by mixing a small amount of iodine in plain baby oil. Shake well to mix. It is a cheap tanning mix and is probably as effective as any of the commercial brands.

Above the ten thousand foot level, I would warn against using any kind of *tanning* lotion, even for those with relatively dark complexions.

Above this elevation, the intensity of the ultraviolet rays is so great that the only protection one can count on is that obtained by using an *opaque cream.* While there are several commercial products marketed that do this job, the best is, ironically, the cheapest. It is called zinc oxide U.S.P., and is just that: white zinc oxide suspended in a petroleum jelly manufactured to United States Pharmacopeia specifications. One tube of this mixture (2 oz.) will last several years. It is better than either lip balms or any sun tanning cream at high altitudes, because it completely blocks all ultraviolet rays from your skin. Its whiteness contrasts with the skin and lets you know when it has worn or rubbed off. When covered with this preparation, your skin is usually one hundred percent safe from sunburn.

Another problem which is very common among hikers at high altitudes is dehydration. The air at high altitudes is very low in moisture. This means that water will evaporate off one's clothes and body much faster than one is aware. An average hiker on a mountain trail may be evaporating more than one gallon of perspiration off his body in a single day. Perspiration or sweat, as everyone knows, is that wet sticky stuff that your body produces, and it performs an important function, its odor notwithstanding. It maintains your body temperature at a sufficiently cool level of 98.6° when you are on the trail heating yourself up with your energy output. Sweat, as we also know, contains salt. Since sweating removes salt from the body, profuse sweating such as that which goes on with exertion at high altitudes can desalt the body excessively and dangerously. Such desalting results in feelings of weakness, nausea, and light-headedness. These symptoms indicate the beginning of what is commonly called heat prostration or salt stroke. The cure is simply to drink salt water and rest a couple of hours. To prevent salt stroke it is a good idea to carry a pack of salt tablets with you on the trail. If the day is hot, take a couple of tablets at lunchtime.

Another cue to the onset of salt stroke is that you feel weak and thirsty, but water does not seem to make you feel better. A couple of salt tablets should perk you up. If that does not work, a good hot meal will get you back in fighting form.

Being careful of one's health is always important, but it is especially important at high altitudes. To this end, you should always take special notice of your water intake and the dryness of your skin. Doing so will help ensure your mountain trip of being a successful and comfortable one.

CHAPTER 7

MAPS AND ORIENTATION

Two of the most important items in a good backpacker's pack are his map and his compass. Whether you are traveling on trails or cross country, a good map and a compass are invaluable aids. In mountainous terrain the only maps which accurately depict variations in elevation are topographical maps. Topographical maps show gradations in elevation by means of lines which follow the contours of the terrain. Intervals between the contour lines represent changes in elevation. When such lines are close together, the change in elevation occurs over a short distance and one knows that the terrain is steep. When the distance between contours is great, one knows that the terrain is relatively flat.

In the sample map seen at right one can see that the interval between contour lines in the lower left portion (southwest) of the Imaginary Mountain is very little. One can surmise from this information that it would be very difficult to hike up Imaginary Mountain from this side. If we look to the upper lefthand portion of the map, we can see that the interval between contour lines here is greater, but

Imaginary Mountain

steep

very steep

easy

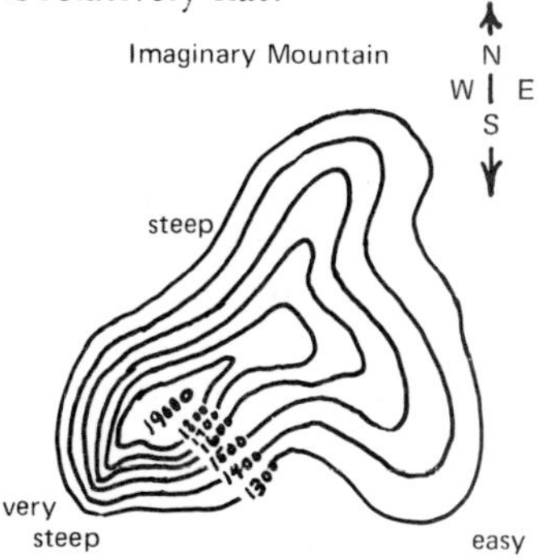

it is still a steep hike up the mountain. The best hiking route up the mountain is, of course, from the southeastern approach (lower right corner) where contour intervals are wide and the hiking easy. A final note of caution should be interjected here: that is, that you must be very careful to read the small contour elevation figures in order to find out whether the elevation is increasing or decreasing in the direction in which you are traveling. A person failing to note such figures on a contour map might mistake a depression area for a mountain area. Experience in reading topographic maps will usually eliminate the possibility of this miscalculation.

The best maps for backpacking are the "15 Minute Series" topographic maps published by the U.S. Geological Survey. These maps not only show variations in elevation, but accurately depict trails, streams, springs, roads, clearings, swamps, mines, structures, and numerous other natural and man-made land forms. They are also printed with a declination chart in the lower left-hand corner to aid in orienting oneself to the terrain with a compass.

These topographic maps are available both from the offices of the U.S. Geological Survey and from their designated dealers. If you are unfamiliar with any dealers in your area, or if the U.S. Geological Survey has no offices in your area, write to one of the following addresses for a 15-Minute Series Index Map of the state in which you will be backpacking.

For states east of the Mississippi:

Washington Distribution Center
U.S. Geological Survey
1200 South Eads Street
Arlington, Virginia 22202

For states west of the Mississippi:

Denver Distribution Center
U.S. Geological Survey
Denver Federal Center, Bldg. 41
Denver, Colorado 80225

The index map that will be sent to you will have enough detail on it for you to choose which maps you want. The reverse side of the index map will also give information about special maps (usually of National Parks) and will list commercial and U.S. Geological Survey distributors in that state. With this information you can either purchase the maps from the aforementioned distributors or you can send your money and the information describing the maps you want back to the appropriate U.S.G.S. Distribution Center.

The 15-Minute Series topographic maps are printed on a scale of 1:24,000, which is quite detailed when one considers that the average road map is printed on a scale of 1:1,000,000. For most circumstances, 15-Minute Series maps provide more than adequate detail. Still, if one desires even more detail, the U.S.G.S. publishes a 7½-Minute Series, which is four times as detailed as the 15-minute maps.

If you are backpacking in a National Forest, it is also a good idea to obtain a special map of the National Forest in which you are traveling. These maps are usually distributed free of charge through the district headquarters of the National Forest that you are visiting. While these maps are inferior to the 15-Minute Series maps (they are not detailed enough), they are often the only thing available for one reason or another, but are usually adequate.

An important reason for carrying good topographic maps along is that they detail all streams and creeks. This is of special importance to late-summer hikers. During the late summer, many streams and springs are dry, and the backpacker must plan his water consumption accordingly. Inferior maps do not show year-round water supplies, and their use can lead one to carry extra water unnecessarily. Water is heavy (1 pint = 1 pound) and should not be carried around needlessly.

Another reason for taking topographical maps is that they are fun. When you get up on top of a mountain or up in a pass, you can see just where you came from and just where you are going. It becomes possible to identify high peaks and lakes which are miles away.

A good map lets you plan your day most conveniently so that you can stop near that bubbling brook at lunchtime. It forewarns you to pass through that mosquito-infested marsh in the crisp morning air when you will not get eaten alive. A detailed topographic map will show you how to get to that "off the beaten path" lake where the trout are sixteen inches and longer.

Last, but not least, that little map in your pack may save your life if you become lost. Better than that though, you will not become lost. All you need is a topographic map and a compass, and the trail is only as far away as your feet.

Always take a compass along. It need not even be a very good one, except that it should have a lock on the needle for when it is not in use. Such compasses can be purchased for a dollar or two, and you need not be a genius to use it.

To orient yourself to your surroundings with a map it is preferable to be standing on a promontory, in a clearing, next to a cliff, or near some type of terrain that is easily distinguished on a topographic map. There are few places in the mountains which are far from such spots. The next step is to lay your map out on the ground next to your compass. Let the compass needle swing until it comes to rest pointing north. Be sure that there are no knives, packframes or other metallic objects near the compass, as they will affect its operation. After the needle comes to rest, bring it alongside the "Declination" diagram in the

left-hand corner of the map. Then turn
the map (not the compass) until "MN"
(magnetic north) on the declination diagram lines up parallel with the needle
on the compass. Then turn the compass until the star on the map lines up
parallel to the "N" (true north) on the
compass.

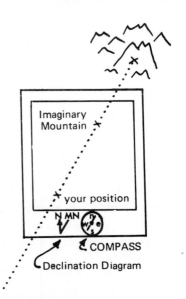

If you are standing on a promontory or are next to a lake, identify
your position on the map and mark it
with a pebble. Then, looking at the
map, identify a nearby cliff or mountain peak and place a pebble on that
point. Then align the two pebbles visu-
ally, and look up. What you are looking at on the map should be staring
you in the face.

Orienting yourself, using two or three of these sightings, will give
you much information, such as where you are going, where trails will
meet, how far away the trail is, etc. Practicing this simple exercise develops one's map reading abilities, develops a familiarity with the scale of
the map, and teaches you how to navigate across country without trails.

If one is lost, it is only a bit more difficult to find out where you
are. As always, it is easier to identify your position if you are standing
atop a promontory or next to a lake. Do not attempt to climb a promontory or scale a cliff in the late afternoon. If you are lost at this time
of day, lie low. Climbing down off a mountain or cliff in the dark can
be extremely dangerous. Stay low, make a campfire and wait until
morning. When atop the promontory the next morning, align your map
and compass as explained before. Then look around you for landmarks
such as lakes, outstanding mountain peaks, bluffs, canyons, or unfor-
ested areas. Being very careful, compare the physiographic features of
the land with the features on the map. Such careful observation should
allow you to identify at least two or more prominent land forms. Com-
paring the distance between these land forms to your own distance from
them should enable you to determine your position and the distance
and direction to the nearest trail or road.

If this method of orientation fails, or if no promontories are available for sightings, do not panic. Stay calm and use your head.

At this point there are two things that you can do. First, you can find a clearing or lake and stay put until you are rescued. Rescue aircraft are always on the watch for smoke, so keep a campfire going at all times and keep plenty of firewood handy. If you are near a clearing, pattern an S O S signal into the grass with fire or stones.

A second method of rescue is, to my mind, more practical. That is, to find a river and follow it downstream till it meets a town, trail crossing or highway bridge. Also, most heavily wooded areas have fire-break roads that one can follow down to a hunting lodge road and from there to a main road.

Few backpackers ever become really "lost." Keeping track of your progress on a map will always give you some idea of where you are. Even the most careless backpacker will have some vague idea of his general location if he has a map and compass.

Be smart. Always carry these two items. Learning how to use a map and compass is quite simple. Maps can save you much hardship and can possibly save your life. Knowing how to use a map is as important to a backpacker as knowing how to travel light. It is a skill which should be familiar to all woodsmen.

A final word of caution is in order here. It is not uncommon to find a person who will mark out his backwoods expedition on the standard topographic maps and just take off. Such an outing can easily turn out disastrously. Our intrepid backpacker might find out that bridges which he assumed existed had been washed out the previous spring. He might find that those easy cross-country treks are extremely difficult, or that streams which he assumed were running turn out to be bone dry. Such a disastrous outing can be avoided by merely consulting the local National Park or forest ranger. He can tell you how the streams are running; how the scenery is; how the weather will be; how the mosquitos are biting; and most important of all, whether you are planning a longer hike than you can comfortably handle.

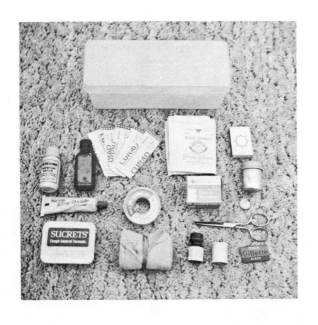

CHAPTER 8

FIRST AID AND MOUNTAIN MEDICINE

Nothing could pertain more to mountain backpacking than the old Boy Scout motto, "Be Prepared." While injuries and illness are rarities on backpacking trips, one should always be adequately prepared to deal with such emergencies.

The best way to deal with distress situations is to avoid them. The best way to do this is to use your common sense. Do not push your own limits. If you have altitude sickness, do not press on toward the summit. If you are tired, do not press on toward another campsite. If you have a sore throat or cold, do not press on toward doing ten miles when you are tired after five. If you have a seven-day hike planned, do not try to average fifteen miles a day. Common sense and a cool head are your best friends in the mountains. Your body has certain limits, but do not press those limits. Hold on to your reserve energy, so that when you need it, it will be there.

A most important factor in dealing with the wilderness environment is learning about it. While this book intends to give a few hints about coping with nature, it is in no sense comprehensive. Your best protection in the wilds is a good working knowledge of nature. Lack of such knowledge leads to fear, and fear is but one step away from panic. Panic will be your worst enemy in distress situations. Above all else, keep a cool head and respect the elements. The mountains of the west have claimed the lives of those who have foolishly defied nature's power. It is not "sissy" to turn back from a mountain climb if an electrical storm is moving in. Nor is it "chicken" to tie a safety line around yourself when fording a swift stream. Unlike the train coming down the tracks, nature will not warn you of her fury; so be prepared.

One way to be prepared is to carry an adequate first aid kit should an accident occur. An adequate first aid kit for a backpacking trip will not be found in a neat prepackaged container on your druggist's shelf. Such pre-packaged containers are made for use around the home and auto where professional care is but a few minutes distant. An adequate first aid kit for a backpacking trip must be assembled with the realization that professional help is at best several hours distant. Regardless of the number of persons along on an outing, every group should carry all of the following items:

1. BANDAIDS — will be the most frequently used item in the kit. Take about five per person on a week-long trip.

2. IODINE — is by far the best disinfectant for small wounds. If you don't like iodine, use a first aid cream (mercurochrome's value as a disinfectant is minimal).

3. ADHESIVE TAPE — is always good to have along for minor emergencies like fixing broken glasses and tying things together. Its use on blisters is discussed in chapter two (Shoes and Foot Care). Adhesive tape is a virtual necessity for securing dressings.

4. STERILE GAUZE PADS — in sizes 3" X 3" or 4" X 4" are a must for dressing large wounds and cuts.

5. STERILE GAUZE ROLL — is also a must for dressing large wounds or securing a dressing. The most convenient size is the 10 yd 1 inch size.

6. BURN CREAM OR VASELINE — is necessary for treating burns. A small tube is adequate.

7. PILLS AND TABLETS should include:

Salt tablets — use is explained in chapter 6, page 74.

Vitamin C tablets — to ward off infections and supplement diet deficiency.

Halozone or Iodine Tabs — for purifying questionable water. Plain iodine can also be used. Wait 30 minutes before drinking treated water.

8. SCISSORS OR RAZOR BLADE — can be used to cut dressings or adhesive tape. They can also be used to cut hair away from a scalp wound for dressing.

9. NEEDLE & THREAD — can be used for piercing a blister. Thread always comes in handy for sewing up a torn garment, and can even be used to sew up skin in an emergency, if the needle is sharp enough.

10. MATCHES — preferably dipped in parafin or in a waterproof case, might be carried in event other matches are ruined by a dip in the drink.

11. SNAKE BITE KIT — should be carried when it is known that poisonous snakes are present. Supreme care must be taken in its use. Read the directions carefully, and do not cut too deep. Doctors have found that often more damage is done to the victim by the first aider than by the snake. First aiders in their zeal often cut too deep into the flesh, severing nerves. One good rule to follow is: NEVER CUT ACROSS an arm or leg (you may sever an artery or vein); CUT LENGTHWISE.

12. LIP BALM — for protecting lips from sun and wind.

13. ACE BANDAGE — can be handy in case of sprains or strained muscles. If sterilized, it can also be used as a bandage.

The following items are not routinely necessary, but can be helpful in distress situations:

1. PILLS AND TABLETS CAN INCLUDE:

Aspirin — for headaches, pain relief, and fever control.

Cold tablets or decongestants — if anyone comes down with hay fever.

Antacid tablets — such as Milk of Magnesia or other commercial preparations to counteract stomach distress.

2. TRIANGLE BANDAGE — can be helpful for bandaging head injuries or restraining a broken arm. Do not use a triangle bandage as a tourniquet. Untrained use of a tourniquet can be more detrimental than helpful. Stop bleeding by direct pressure on the wound. A tourniquet should be used only as a last resort.

3. ZINC OXIDE OINTMENT — this opaque cream provides very good skin protection at high altitudes. See page 72.

4. MOLESKIN — is preferred by some for use on blisters.

5. GERMICIDAL SOAP — is preferred by some persons to iodine, as it does not sting. Use liberally in cleaning cuts prior to dressing.

6. FOOT POWDER — for protecting feet against athlete's foot.

7. LAXATIVES — Dried fruit eaten along the way generally suffices, but for those who have in the past had uncomfortable experiences, carrying their own herbal remedies would be advised.

Hopefully you will never have to use your first aid kit, but should the need arise, be sure that it is ready and that you know how to use it. If you do not have any background in giving first aid, obtain a copy of the American National Red Cross' First Aid Textbook. This book is crammed with easy-to-read information on dealing with emergency situations. It is strongly recommended. The Red Cross also offers first aid classes in most major cities.

Accidents and illness on backpacking trips are frequently the result of bull-headedness and stupidity. Do not tempt fate by taking unnecessary risks. For instance, many backpackers do not realize that eating burnt food or drinking burnt cocoa or chocolate can cause serious stomach upsets; however, a little knowledge goes a long way in preventing all sorts of emergencies.

One unnecessary risk that many backpackers take is that of drinking water that could be contaminated. One should never be overly confident of the purity of any water. Most backpacking is done in National Parks and in U.S. Forest Service wilderness areas where water purity standards are extremely high. Still, whenever you have even the slightest suspicion of water contamination, treat your water with halozone or iodine tablets. Such suspicion would apply:

1. Whenever cattle are grazing on the watershed.
2. Whenever camped on a watershed with many other campers.
3. Whenever water has a scum on it.
4. Whenever detergent bubbles are found in calm waters.
5. Whenever the water has poor clarity.
6. Whenever there is evidence that the water has been sitting in one place for a long time.
7. Whenever water has an odor or strange taste to it ⎫ Do not ingest
8. Whenever there is no life whatsoever in the water. ⎰ even if treated

Do not take chances with the water you drink. Tainted water can make you very sick. Even a simple case of dysentery can lay you low and ruin an otherwise enjoyable trip.

Another cardinal rule is that you should never go swimming alone. Mountain waters can harbor unforeseen dangers.

Several years ago, while I was on a trip up Lyell Canyon in Yosemite National Park with two friends, we decided to stop for a midmorning dip in a pool of glistening water. We knew that the water was coming out of the Lyell Glacier at the head of the canyon and that it was c-o-l-d. Still, we were dirty with sweat and couldn't have cared less. We all waded out into the pool, and it was indeed very cold. My hearty friends then proceeded to start swimming farther out into the pool and beckoned me to follow. I followed obediently, but on the first stroke my chest muscles tightened so that I couldn't breathe. The muscles had rebelled against the cold water. Fortunately, my friends detected my distress and helped me to shore, where I slowly recovered my breath.

I relate this story to the reader to demonstrate that the dangers that lie along the trail are not always obvious. Caution is the most reasonable course in unfamiliar situations. The intelligent backpacker takes no unnecessary chances, and more often than not leaves his first aid kit in the bottom of his packbag for the entire trip.

Mosquitoes—How to Relax and Enjoy Yourself

One mid-July day while on a day-hike up through the woods above Tuolumne Meadows (Yosemite National Park), my friend and I met a church group coming down the mountain from one of Yosemite's lakes. The members of this group, numbering about fifty, staggered down the trail like a defeated army. They had done battle with the mosquitoes of Yosemite and had lost. All had severe bites about the extremities, and several had their eyes swollen shut by bites they had received. It was truly a sorry sight. It was all the more sorry when I thought of the bad impression Mother Nature had left with them.

This disaster could have been averted had the leaders of this group prepared the trip properly and done some investigating beforehand.

To understand why this group met with such an uncomfortable situation, we must learn a few things about the life cycle of the mosquito in the mountains.

Mosquitoes are water animals. They breed in water and they live around water. Thus, where you find water you will find mosquitoes. And when you find stagnant water, such as is found in mountain bogs and marshes, you will find many mosquitoes.

The second thing we must know is that the presence of mosquitoes is a cyclical phenomenon which is quite predictable. The presence of large numbers of mosquitoes is dependent on the quantity of water present and the season of the year.

Anyone who has spent much time in the mountains knows that the winter snows swell the streams in the spring and early summer, but that by September one is lucky to find a trickle here and there.

Since mosquito eggs hatch according to temperature and water conditions, even a novice entomologist can accurately predict the cyclic changes in mosquito populations.

The mosquitoes with which mountain travelers are most familiar are members of the genus *Aedes*. The various species and subspecies of this group of mosquitoes lay their eggs in shallow water or in wet boggy soil. The eggs of these mosquitoes can be frozen, and indeed are, during the winter months. During the cold months the eggs lie dormant. Hatching occurs only when the ice in which they are immersed melts and the correct temperature conditions occur. Scientists know that the actual hatching is triggered by variations in the air and water temperatures. Both factors (correct air temperatures and water availability) must be present and the temperatures of both must be raised to a specific level to trigger the hatching of the eggs. Eggs of the genus *Aedes* share the common characteristic of requiring relatively high air and water temperatures to trigger hatching.

Because the eggs need such temperatures in order to hatch, one will rarely find mosquitoes in the western mountains until April or May.

Before these months, the eggs are covered with snow and the air remains too cold for hatching. When June rolls around, breeding conditions are ideal and mosquitoes are most abundant. The ground is sodden with the melted snows of the past winter and air temperatures are high. This condition often continues through June and into July. Toward the end of July, the ground begins to dry and fewer mosquito eggs hatch. Because the creature lives but three to ten days, the population begins to decrease rapidly. By August they are of little bother to the backpacker.

This is the normal sequence of the "mosquito cycle." It is not, however, a hard-and-fast pattern. Cyclic patterns of mosquito populations vary slightly according to the species and altitude.

As a general rule, the snows higher up in the mountains melt later. Thus, the ground at higher elevations (9,000 feet plus) may be moist and boggy in late July. Consequently, one often finds mosquitoes at higher elevations later in the season than would be expected. Similarly, at lower elevations the ground may dry out in June, and mosquitoes will be virtually nonexistent by mid-July.

The backpacker who uses his head can utilize these facts about the "mosquito cycle" to his own advantage in planning trips. One can avoid the swarms of mosquitoes that exist in the early summer by planning backpacking trips for August and September. If this is not feasible, one can also avoid them by hiking at lower elevations in June and July. This advice may seem absurd, or overly protective, but really it is not!

Only one who has been surrounded by a cloud of mosquitoes in June can truly appreciate the value of this warning. I personally have traveled eight miles in a little over two hours to escape clouds of mosquitoes, and can say that it was not very much fun.

Aside from this timing aspect, there is another good way to avoid the mosquitoes in the mountains, and that is to plan your campsite carefully. Keep your campsite a reasonable distance (at least fifty yards) away from wet soil or swamp water. Such places are likely locales for mosquito swarms. An investigation of potential campsites on your topographical map will usually give you some idea of the potential for mosquito swamps. Avoid camping in places near marshes, or where there is a poor distinction between dry land and water, such as in a "meadow." Mountain meadows are merely lakes which have silted up over a period of time. Because meadows are composed of rich sedimentary soils, they tend to hold water and mosquitoes. Backpackers should avoid camping out in meadows during the early summer. Meadows with poor drainage can support large populations of mosquitoes on into the late summer months.

Mosquitoes can be very bothersome on a backpacking trip or can be no bother at all. I personally am greatly annoyed by them. Some people can ignore swarms of the pesky creatures.

Certainly, one will not plan one's trip with the sole object of avoiding mosquitoes, but it is nevertheless a good policy to avoid looking for trouble. When alternate routes are available, avoid marshes and bogs. Camp near swiftly flowing water if at all possible. When camped near lakes, stay well above the wet shore and expose your campsite to the wind if possible.

The camper who follows these directions and arranges his travels in the late summer months will avoid the fate of the unfortunate church group mentioned earlier.

Still, if all these precautions fail, the modern backpacker has a solid bastion of defense against the evil bloodsuckers of the mountains—that is, of course, insect repellent. Even if the mosquitoes are buzzing around you in swarms, you will not get bitten if you have an adequate insect repellent.

As far as present technology is concerned, there is nothing presently available to the public which will keep mosquitoes from swarming around you. However, there is one chemical which will keep them from biting you: N, N, diethyl-meta-toluamide. This chemical was developed by the Entomology Research Laboratories of the U.S. Department of Agriculture in cooperation with the Army Medical Corps. I will not name brands, but I will say that any insect repellent which does not contain this ingredient is an inferior-grade repellent. This information is readily obtained by carefully reading the label of the container where it says, "Active Ingredients." Consequently, if you buy a commercial brand of insect repellent, you are buying only an odor and N, N, diethyl-meta-toluamide. If you want to smell pretty, buy your repellent at the cosmetic department of your local department store. If you want to prevent insect bites, then read the labels of the insect repellent you buy.

After doing a little checking around, I found out that the repellent with the highest percentage of N, N, diethyl-meta-toluamide was not one of the commercial brands which "smell nice." Of all the commercial brands, the best one contained only 25% of this ingredient. Even though I can attest the relative effectiveness of this brand, two ounces of it cost $1.49 . . . ouch! In other words, the consumer is paying $3.00 an ounce for the active ingredient.

Interestingly enough, I found out how I could purchase this chemical for as little as 30 cents an ounce, and it is readily available. It is known as United States Army Insect Repellent Type IIA. It is available in many Army surplus stores for 39-49 cents for two fluid ounces which contain about 75% N, N, diethyl-meta-toluamide. There is also a type IIB repellent, which contains about 50% of this ingredient, also in a two-ounce bottle. Both are incredibly effective. If one keeps his skin and clothes properly covered (if you miss one spot the mosquitoes will find it), one can be virtually guaranteed of no bites.

For use on clothes, you can dilute with plain rubbing alcohol and splash directly on your clothing. WASH HANDS; AVOID INHALING.

At this point, however, a few notes of caution should be included. Most important, be careful not to get this chemical or any other insect repellent in your eyes. Like most insect repellents, N, N, diethyl-meta-toluamide is a powerful chemical; and if it gets into your eyes, you will experience an uncomfortable itching feeling. If this happens, DO NOT RUB YOUR EYES. Wash your eyes with plain water and *suffer*. Your eyes may become red, but the redness will go away in a day or two.

Also, keep your repellent away from plastic substances like sunglasses, canteens, toothbrushes, and plastic bags. N, N, diethyl-meta-toluamide has the capacity to soften certain plastic compounds. It does not seem to affect nylon or natural cloth substances. I discovered this interesting characteristic when a bottle leaked in my backpack and I found my "melted" toothbrush the next morning. Last, if you are going out in May, June or July, do not be caught with too little insect repellent. Two extra ounces are not going to break your back, and they may save your sanity.

For the ecology-minded backpacker who does not want to use any kind of chemical pesticide, a botanical spray or powder can be made from pyrethrum. This is one of man's oldest and safest insect killers, and is made from the dried heads of chrysanthemums (*Chrysanthemum cinerariaefolium*).

CHAPTER 9

BEARS AND BEAR-PROOFING

Shortly after dark a large black bear followed by two cubs made its way into a campground. Frightened campers making ready for bed shrieked in horror. Some stood a safe distance away and quietly observed the trio of bears. Others fled to their cars in fear for their lives. Suddenly a portly ranger appeared and blocked the path of the large mother bear. He approached her and kicked her in the posterior. The mother bear growled her disapproval, turned around and scampered away into the woods followed closely by her cubs.

In another incident, a black bear followed by two cubs made her way into a campground shortly after dark. This group found what it was looking for: Food. A group of backpackers had carelessly left their food supply on the ground, and Mrs. Black Bear had found it. The startled campers banged on pots and yelled, to no avail. The bears calmly continued to consume the entire food supply. Finally, in a fit of desperation one of the campers tried to pull a bag of food away from the big bear. Not at all pleased with this gesture, the big bear swung a paw at the invader, and severely lacerated the camper's arm.

Which of these incidents reflects the true personality of the black bear? Is the black bear by nature a docile animal that fears people, or is it a wild hunger-crazed beast ready to mutilate anyone that separates it from its goal?

To a certain extent, both of these statements contain some degree of truth. The two incidents cited above are true, and it is not unlikely that they will be repeated in the future.

Black Bear, 5-6'

Grizzly Bear, 6-7'

To a person not attuned to the psychological quirks of a wild animal, it would appear that there is some disparity in the behavior of these two animals of the same species. In reality, this is not true. The bear that walked away in the former incident had not yet found any food and was not, therefore, motivated to argue with the ranger. In the latter incident, the bear had already found food, and having claimed it as her own, was only defending her "rightful" claim. This seemingly minute distinction fully accounts for the vicious behavior of the bear in the latter incident.

Bears and other wild animals do not have the finely developed sense of logic possessed by man, and therefore they do not always react predictably. Furthermore, wild animals are often unaware of their great strength. In fact, the bear that lacerated the camper's arm might only have been trying to scare him away. Unaware of her great power, the animal did far more damage.

It is for these reasons that visitors to our National Parks are warned not to feed or play with the wild animals. Wild animals cannot be depended upon to react favorably to advances upon them by human beings. Furthermore, by feeding bears and other animals, you are doing them no favor. Man's foods do no good for the digestive tracts of these animals. Similarly, the feeding of offspring distracts the mother from her job of teaching them to seek natural forage.

There are two species of bear in the western United States. There is the Grizzly (*Ursus horribilis*), whose range extends from the Colorado Rockies north into Alaska. And there is the black bear (*Euarctos americanus*), which inhabits nearly every mountain range in the west.

Most backpackers will never see a grizzly bear, as most of them were killed off in the nineteenth and early twentieth centuries. Most grizzlies alive today in the western United States live in the National Parks and remote wilderness areas of Wyoming, Idaho and Montana. Recent estimates indicate that there are fewer than one thousand grizzlies remaining in the United States outside of Alaska.

The National Park Service of the United States Department of the Interior has published an excellent booklet entitled, "In Grizzly Country." This booklet has been written especially for persons going into the backcountry. Because this booklet has limited availability, I have decided to reproduce a few highly informative paragraphs herein.

BEAR FACTS

An adult grizzly bear will stand six to seven feet high. His coat may range in color from yellowish to dark brown or nearly black. Usually his hairs are tipped with white, giving him a frosty or grizzled look.

The grizzly has a dished, or concave, face; long, curved, exposed claws on his front feet and a distinguishing hump above his shoulders.

Grizzlies are rarely seen except in the back country. Even there, they are not a common sight. But, if you are in bear country, be on the alert and take some precautions. Have some idea what to do, based on the experience of others, in case you come face to face with a bear.

Don't hike alone in bear country. Stay with a group. Watch for bear droppings, tracks and diggings. They are signs there have been bears around. If you see one at a distance, make a wide detour around it, keeping up wind so the bear will get your scent and know you are there. If you can't detour, wait until the bear moves away from your route. The rule is to stay as far away from the animal as possible.

Under most circumstances, bears avoid people, so it is a good idea to make your presence known. That's why experienced hikers wear bells or put some pebbles in a tin can to rattle as they walk. Whistling and loud talking are other ways to signal your presence. However, noise is not a foolproof way of avoiding them.

What should you do if you are suddenly confronted by a grizzly? Whatever you do, try to remain calm.

If the grizzly is not aggressive and merely stands its ground, probably you should stand still too. Don't run! This frequently excites the bear into pursuit. Do not move toward the bear. It may feel you are invading its territory and react accordingly. The animal may simply be curious about the noise and waiting until the source comes into the focus of its weak eyes.

A grizzly will often rise on its hind legs. If it does, it may be effective to speak softly to the animal. Steady, soft human monotones often appear effective in assuring bears that no harm is meant to them. However, while standing your ground and speaking softly, look for a tree to climb.

If the animal advances aggressively, your next move depends on the distance to the tree, which ought to be tall enough to get you out of reach of the bear (only young grizzlies can climb trees). As a delaying action it might help to drop some sizeable item—a bedroll or camera for instance) which may divert the bear and give you more time to retreat. If you can get up a tree, stay there until you are certain the bear is out of the area. If you can't reach a tree, and the bear continues to advance, your best bet may be to play dead, lying on your stomach or on your side with your legs drawn up to your chest. Clasp your hands over the back of your neck. Grizzlies have passed by people in this position without harming them.

Others have been only slightly injured when the bear made one or two halfhearted slaps at them. Never harass a bear unless it is actually physically attacking someone. In such an emergency, try to distract the bear from its victims by shouting or throwing sticks and stones. In any event, don't run blindly down the trail or through the brush, hoping to outdistance the bear. It will only excite the animal. Besides, a human can never expect to outrun a bear, especially in rugged terrain.

A mother grizzly with cubs is a special hazard. Most of the serious attacks in parks have occurred when people inadvertently have come upon a female with her cubs. The mother's natural protective instinct is highly developed, and she looks upon intruders as a threat to her family. She may attack, seemingly without provocation, charging and slapping her forepaws at the nearest person and then passing on to others. If the human intruders have dropped to the ground to play dead, the bear may sniff each one and perhaps claw and bite them before moving her cubs to safety. Lying still under the jaws of a biting bear takes a lot of courage, but it may prevent greater injury or death. Resistance normally would be useless.

Back-country camping requires special precautions. An area frequented by bears is the wrong place to pitch a tent. So is a foot or animal trail. Bears travel on trails too, especially at night. Try to camp where there are trees handy. Campers must not throw away garbage or trash nor shall they bury garbage or food containers. Combustible trash should go in the fire. Tin cans and other noncombustible trash, except glass, should also be burned to destroy food odors. The cans must then be removed from the cold ashes, flattened, and transported out to the trailhead in plastic bags for deposit in trash containers.

Foodstuffs should be stored (preferably packaged in plastic) out of the reach of bears. Food can be suspended by ropes between two trees. If previous campers have left a dirty camp, clean up the mess for your own protection. Use dry, pre-packaged foods and avoid greasy, odorous foods such as bacon and ham. It's best not to sleep in the clothes you wore when cooking. Packs and sleeping bags should be kept clean and free of food odors. As a precaution against the presence of these odors, sleep some distance from your campfire and cooking area.

PACK OUT WASTE YOU CAN'T BURN IN YOUR CAMPFIRE.

Special precautions apply to women. For their protection, women should stay out of the back country during their menstrual periods. Bears and other large animals have attacked women in this physiological condition. Perfumes, hair sprays, deodorants and cosmetics should not be used or carried into the back country. There is some evidence that bears have been attracted and infuriated by these scents.

The more frequently encountered black bear is considerably smaller than his larger cousin. He generally weighs about 400 pounds fully grown. The black bear is classified by scientists as an omnivorous animal, meaning that it will eat both flesh and plants. Despite this classification, "Blackie" is mostly a vegetarian. His flesh-eating classification is regarded as generally inaccurate by experts on black bears. The black

bear's indulgence in meat is generally the result of his stealing the remains of another animal's kill or surprising an old squirrel as he comes out of his burrow in the ground.

The black bear is not necessarily black, and in most cases is not. His color may be cinnamon brown or even tan. There is no such thing as a "cinnamon bear." Such cinnamon-colored bears are merely local variations in the coloring of the common black bear. All such animals are members of the same species.

Aside from sheer size, the easiest way to distinguish between the black bear and the grizzly is to look at the tracks or forefeet of the animal. The black bear has a five-padded foot with small claws extending forward of the pads slightly. The grizzly has the same five pads, but his claws are considerably longer, extending three to four inches in front of the pads.

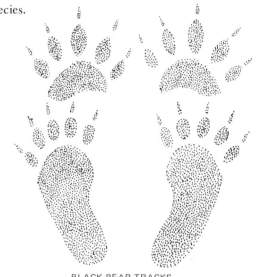

BLACK BEAR TRACKS

Black bears can climb trees and, in fact, regard them as their natural retreat when attacked. So do not bother to climb a tree if you see a black bear. Just give "Blackie" a wide berth and you will be quite safe. Black bears are not considered ferocious animals and will rarely, if ever, attack a human being unless provoked.

Still, a bear like any other creature is a hungry beast. If the pickin's are good he is going to be the first one in line, and backpackers' food stores are easy pickin's. Thus, one must take precautions to safeguard his food supply. Needless to say, protection of one's food can be of crucial importance when one is several days away from civilization on foot.

There is no completely foolproof method of preventing bears from getting at your food, for there are few things that man can do that a black bear cannot undo. Furthermore, bears have a very good sense of smell. How then can one protect himself from having his food consumed by an ungrateful bear?

By far the best method is to carry a large tin can. At night place all food in this can and bury it. But do not bury it just anyplace. Bury it right under where you are going to sleep. This method is virtually 100% safe, but it is also too tedious for most people. In most cases, such burial is only used for caching food for a return trip or later pickup.

With this in mind, I will suggest the second and most widely used method of bear-proofing—the tree-hang. In this method the food is tied up high in a tree in hopes that a bear will not see it or smell it.

For this method you must carry along 50-60 feet of nylon clothesline cord and a stuff bag or plastic bag. Together these should weigh no more than 5-6 oz. Then single out the largest tree in the area of your camp. Such a tree will undoubtedly have some long limbs. Tie a small rock to the end of the line, being careful not to tangle it; throw it over the highest limb that you can reach, the higher the better. Also, the farther out on that limb, the better. Do not forget to hold the free end of the cord, or you might lose it and wind up without anything to hang your food up with. Take care that (1) the rock does not come back down and hit you; (2) the limb is strong enough that it doesn't break off and hit you on the head. Work the cord as far out on the limb as you dare, then put the food in the bag and hoist it up. Leave it suspended far enough below the limb (two feet or so) that squirrels do not dare jump down to it. Then take the free end of the cord and tie it to another tree as high up on the trunk as you can reach.

If the food is 25-30 feet off the ground in a clean plastic bag, even the keen sense of smell of a bear should not detect it. And since a bear's eyes are not the best, he should not detect your lead line. So far, this system has worked for me, but I will not give any guarantees.

Some persons use another system for storing their food at night. They suspend their food from a bar tied between two trees. For several

reasons, I think that this system is less desirable than the aforementioned procedure: (1) First, it is too hard to rig up a bar high enough that it is out of the bears' range of climbing. (2) Second, if *you* can climb that high in a tree to rig up a bar, the bear probably can too. (3) Last, it is too much trouble unless one plans a long stay at the campground.

A final word is in order here. I find it a good practice to take a flashlight (if you have one) and your *clean* pots and pans to bed with you. Between clanging the pots together, your loud shouting, and the flashlight, any roving bear who has not already got his grubby paws on your food is likely to be scared out of his mind. If he finds your food, though, forget it. Once Mr. Bear tastes the delicious dried fruit, the scintillating salt and the crispy crackers, only a bulldozer can move him, so don't try. Let him eat, and you can be sure he will eat it all. Better to save your neck and try to bum food off other backpackers on the trail than to risk personal injury. Backpackers are universally sympathetic to those who have suffered ill-fortune and will undoubtedly come up with a little grub for you. As a final warning: NEVER take food into your sleeping bag with you. A bear can smell it and will try to get it.

Finally, bears seldom wander above the tree line. Once above this elevation, the only threats to one's food stores are marmots and ground squirrels. Both of these animals tend to keep their distance from man. So, my advice on storing food above the tree line is to put it inside your backpack and sleep with your pack right next to you.

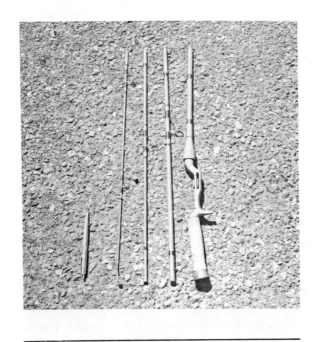

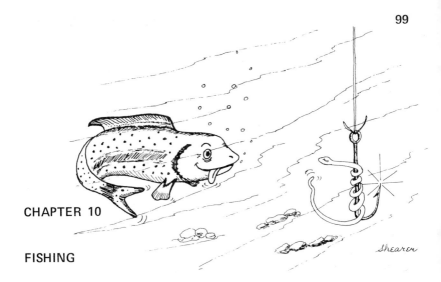

Shearer

CHAPTER 10

FISHING

The mountains offer a wealth of pleasure for those who love to fish. In the western states, out-of-the-way lakes are stocked according to use, and an abundant supply is usually waiting for the backpacker-fisherman. Often, an out-of-the-way lake will contain thousands of fish and nobody will be trying to catch them but you.

Fishing not only provides a welcome respite from the tedium of hiking with a heavy pack, but it also provides a good way to supplement your diet. The finest restaurant's trout menu can rarely surpass fresh mountain "trout in a pan." There is something about a trout that you caught yourself that just makes it taste better.

Even a person who has never fished before should seriously consider buying some fishing gear before heading for the mountains. Too often a non-fisherman is discouraged from taking up the sport because the veteran of the sport describes it as if it were a sacred art. To the layman, fishing is a great mysterious rite. Members of the cult converse with each other about their successes and speak in words unknown to the layman. The mystery aura is further intensified by the layman's visit to a fishing store, where he is presented with countless varieties of bait and hundreds of flies and lures. To the uninitiated, logic dictates that most of these items are entirely useless and that there must be one "ultimate bait." The sanctity of the cult is confirmed when you find out the cost of those items that the salesman says you will "need." The combination of these experiences will generally deter all but the most determined non-member of this exclusive cult.

In reality there is no secret to getting fish out of a lake or stream. Those strange conversations between members of the cult are no more than exercises in the ancient art of "slinging the bull." And the countless items in the store are merely novelties which the shopkeeper displays in order to separate the fisherman from his money.

Trout fishing is actually the easiest thing in the world. A trout fisherman is actually only a trout psychologist. The trout fisherman does no more than out-smart the trout. The only thing that a trout fisherman does is fool poor, dumb little fish. He fools them by presenting these not-so-intelligent animals with a hook that is disguised as food. The fish takes the disguised hook, and you take your trout.

An experienced fisherman will doubtless be appalled by the above explanation, but in reality there is no secret to trout fishing. It is both easy and fun.

Fishermen divide themselves into two groups, according to the equipment they use. There are two basic types of trout-fishing outfits presently in use, the fly outfit and the spin outfit.

The fly-fishing outfit consists of a very lightweight rod and reel. Fish are caught on imitation flies (with a hook in the middle). These flies are cast upon the water and float on or just below the surface. Fish feeding on the surface mistake them for food and the catch is made.

Spin fishing outfits consist of a heavier rod and reel combination. Fish are caught on (1) hooks which are camouflaged with bait food, (2) artificial lures which resemble bait food or (3) flies set on a line as mentioned above.

Generally speaking, an experienced fly fisherman will always catch more fish than a spin fisherman, but an inexperienced fly fisherman will probably catch fewer fish than an inexperienced spin fisherman.

Since both outfits cost about the same, I would recommend a spin outfit to a beginner. It is easier to use and requires little skill.

Once the average fisherman has his rod and reel, the opportunities for acquiring and using accessory gear are almost unlimited. The backpacking fisherman, however, must be more prudent in his choice of gear. Fishing gear can be very bulky and can mount up faster than you think.

If you are fly fishing, do not take your entire fly collection. Find out what fish are found in the area to which you are going, and then take only the appropriate flies. Leader lines can be wound on thread spools or placed in plastic packets, and fly dope can be put in small leakproof plastic jars.

If you have a spin outfit, do not go overboard with lures. Take only a couple. Many persons like the "Super Duper," but you will usually get better results with salmon eggs and worms (or even cheese!). Take small hooks, never bigger than size 12. Spinners might want to take a couple of dry flies and a fly "bobber" so that they can get fish while they are biting at the surface of a stream.

The hardest problem for the back-country fisherman is how to bring the rod along. In response to this need at least two manufacturers of fishing equipment have designed a backpacker's rod that breaks down into very small sections that can fit inside your pack. Another company makes a rod which telescopes into itself and weighs only a few ounces.

Still, there is an easy way of carrying a regular pole, provided that it breaks down into two sections of reasonable length.

First, get an old baby sock or one of small size. Place a grommet or sew an eyelet in it so that a string can be strung through it. Tie the sock

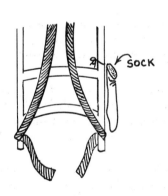

on the pack to one of the frame's lower crossbars, being careful that the toe does not extend below the bottom of the frame. Place the pole sections in the sock and secure them to the vertical frame member with either string or rubber bands. Rubber bands hold the pole sections to the frame more firmly and do not let them rattle. Such an arrangement is lightweight and lets you get at the rod quickly when you want it.

Reels and gear should go inside the pack, or in an outside pocket.

Now that you have your gear together and are up in the mountains, how should you go about catching your evening meal?

LAKE FISHING — When fishing in a lake, keep your fly or bait moving, preferably in short quick movements. If you are fishing with bait on the bottom and feel a "hit," give a slight tug on your line to set the hook into the fish. If the hook did not "set," wait a few seconds, as the fish might come back again. If using flies, cast where you can see the fish rising to take flies at the surface. The best time to catch trout is in the early evening or morning. This is when trout feed most actively.

STREAM FISHING — This kind of fishing is much more challenging than lake fishing. In some ways it is much easier to catch fish in a stream; in other ways it is considerably harder. The best advantage to fishing in a stream is that you can often see the fish that you are trying to catch. It would be hard to equal an advantage like that.

The first step in stream fishing is finding a place to fish. To do this, walk up or down the stream where you are camped, looking carefully into the pools for fish. Be reasonably stealthy. Approach each pool from the side and look into the depression at the head of it. Fish generally congregate at the head of the pool where insects and food are washed down to them from the stream above. Do not be afraid to look closely or even scare the trout into movement. Often you cannot see a trout in the water until it moves. Trout can see relatively well and will probably flee when they see you. Do not for a minute think that you have permanently scared a trout away because it has seen you. They are forgetful animals, and a trout will not remember why it ran for shelter after two or three minutes.

Once you spot a pool where several good-sized trout are congregating, back away and ready your gear. Once your gear is ready, move in closer but only to the point where you can barely see the trout in the pool. Then cast.

Flies can be cast right into the middle or can be entered slightly upstream and allowed to float down. Fly fishermen should learn to keep their lines taut enough that if the fish goes for the lure, the line can be tugged to set the hook. Many a fish has been lost because the line was too loose at the wrong moment.

A spin fishermen should drop his bait or lure right in the middle of a school. If it scares the fish away, leave it still for a moment. Trout are curious creatures and will come back to look at it. If the trout ignore the lure's entry into the water, start reeling it in very slowly. The movement of the object through the water will usually arouse curiosity. Usually a fish will look around the object before it bites. If you see a trout approach the bait, leave it still for a moment. Jerk the line only after the fish has put the bait in its mouth.

Unfortunately, having a fish on a hook is a lot different from having one in a pan. It is quite easy to land a trout if one has a strong line and a net, but the cool clear waters of mountain streams often dictate that the angler must use a very light leader line (fine line going from the regular casting line to the hook). This is generally of lighter weight, so that the fish will not see the line attached to the bait. Furthermore, it is usually foolish for a backpacker to carry the additional weight of a landing net. As a consequence of these two factors, the backpacker-fisherman must be very careful in landing his catch.

Once you have your fish on the hook, do not start dragging him in unless it is a very small trout. After you have given a slight yank on the hook, let the trout make the next move. If you try to pull straight away on the line, the trout's quick jerk might break the leader or unseat the hook. Let the trout make the first move. Chances are that he will turn his body away from you (sidewise) and thereby seat the hook deeper into his flesh. After this first jerk, play the trout. Let it move freely while you slowly reel the line in. Stop reeling if it starts to fight violently, then resume as soon as it stops. Stop reeling when you have about ten feet of line left between the rod tip and the fish. This ten feet allows the springy rod to prevent the line from breaking should the fish try to jerk away suddenly. Then just pull the fish up on the shore, keeping it on the ground at all times. Continue pulling it onto the shore until it is five to ten feet away from the water. Then grasp the fish behind the head and remove the hook. Move away from the pool to carry this out so that the remaining fish will not be disturbed.

In remote areas it is permissible to clean trout directly in the stream from which they were caught. The remains will be eaten by other trout or will be destroyed by bacteria. This should not be done in areas where other backpackers are camped. Such pollution does not ruin the quality of the water, but it is unsightly and should be avoided when other campers are in the area. In such areas, clean the fish away from the stream, dig a hole and bury the remains.

Only a jackknife is needed for cleaning fish. Grasp the fish firmly and run the edge of your knife in forward sweeps along the body. This cleans off the scales. Keep this up under running water until the knife edge runs smoothly along the sides and top surface of the fish. The next step is to slit the underbelly of the trout from just in back of the head to the anus. Then empty out the entrails. Some persons also like to clean out the dorsal (back) vein which runs against the backbone, but this operation is not necessary.

The final step is to cook your catch.

Almost all backpackers have their own special methods of preparing trout, but I picked up a recipe several years ago that is, to my palate, the best of all. It goes like this:

Place about 1/5 to 1/8 cup of pancake batter (per fish) in a bowl or pot. Add beer or water very slowly and stir until a thick creamy consistency is achieved. (Note: it is best to use beer, but water will also yield excellent results.) In a separate plate, chop up several juicy wild onions.* Dip the trout in the batter and sprinkle with onions. Then fry in a liberally greased pan. The results are outstanding. Another good method is to cook the fish on a grill right over the fire. Cook the trout until the outer skin *appears* burned on both sides. Then eat.—*Bon appetit!*

*This plant is usually found growing in mountain marshes and next to streams. Use your nose to find it. The leaves of the wild onion look like blades of grass. (See illustration.)

CHAPTER 11

Shearer

PRESERVING THE MOUNTAIN ECOLOGY

A real backpacker is one who is concerned about the wilderness. He treats it with care, never disturbing or destroying it. He leaves the refuse of civilization beyond the boundaries of the mountains. Indeed, a good backpacker subscribes to the United States Forest Service's admonition to, "Take only pictures, leave only footprints."

In the first chapter of this book, I alluded to the fact that the sport of wilderness backpacking has grown with incredible speed in the last few years. Some persons, including the author, welcome this growth. But there are many veteran backpackers who see the newcomers to the sport as a threat to the future of our wilderness areas, and they are not unfounded in their apprehensions. Newcomers to the sport have failed to treat our wilderness areas with care for their ecology and consideration for their fellow backpackers. Through ignorance, laziness and imprudence they have caused streams to become fouled, trails to be littered, trees to be killed, and animals to be poisoned.

In their wake, novice backpackers leave civilization's waste, and a little less enjoyment for those who follow. The clean campsite which they enjoyed will not be enjoyed by those who follow. The clear bubbly pools in which they washed will not be as clean for those who follow. Of course, such inconsiderate backpackers are not an altogether recent innovation. They have existed for years, but years ago their numbers were few. Fellow backpackers picked up their trash and the streams flushed themselves out eventually. Today, however, these inconsiderate

persons are leaving their wastes behind in such tremendous quantities
that it has sometimes become impossible to keep the woods clean.

This has become a very serious problem in many wilderness areas
and National Parks. The worst example of such environmental abuse by
backpackers is seen in Inyo National Forest, California, in the Lone Pine
Creek watershed. The back-country trail that runs through this watershed leads hikers to the top of Mount Whitney. Because Mt. Whitney is
advertised as the highest point in the lower forty-eight states, and because there is a fine 10½-mile trail to the summit, this "hike to the top"
has become increasingly popular among novice backpackers. In recent
years many thousands of these backpackers have taken the hike to the
top. In their scramble up through the watershed, they have left their
waste and pollution to the extent that the ecology of the watershed has
been seriously threatened. Lakes have become polluted and pools along
the creek have become repositories for detergent bubbles. All deadwood
lying on the ground has long since been burned. Many of the lower
limbs of live trees have been cut off for firewood, leaving them open to
disease. Many deer and other large mammals have left the watershed in
quest of better forage. The trail has become eroded in places by
hikers shortcutting switchbacks. Moreover, everywhere one looks he can
see litter. It is seen along the trail, under rocks, in campfires, behind
bushes—everywhere. Even at the summit one need not look far to see
litter stuck between rocks. Finally, what else need one see to know that
civilization has indeed come to the summit of Mt. Whitney? Yes, you
might have guessed it: spray painted on the summit's boulders, "John
Smith 1975."

What is happening to nature in this wilderness area then is that she
is slowly being either pushed back or destroyed. Through carelessness,
ignorance and naivete, man is gradually destroying the beauty of this
10½-mile stretch of wilderness.

Of course, any wilderness area exposed to the traffic that Lone
Pine Creek watershed has received is bound to suffer some damage.
However, the sad part is that most of the damage to this area and other
areas could have been avoided if campers had only exercised a little bit
of care in their camping habits.

Most apparent among the problems created by novice campers is
that of litter. They litter along the trail and at their campsites. There is
absolutely no excuse for not carrying your nonburnable litter out of
the woods with you. If you can carry it in, you can carry it out. This includes glass, tin cans, and foil in any form. Tin cans can easily be crushed
into a flat shape on a rock, by pounding with another rock.

In the old days campers used to burn and bury their cans. The burning was supposed to kill the scent of the food that was in the can so that bears would not dig the cans up in quest of food. But years of experience have shown that they dig the cans up anyway. So carry them out. Also carry out foil. Do not throw it in the campfire, as it will not burn and it will not rust away for decades. *The use of wilderness areas is so much in demand today that it is becoming more and more imperative that people carry out every last bit of nonburnable trash that they bring in with them.*

Another major problem is that of water pollution. *Backpackers can help solve this problem by using only soap or an organic, biodegradable cleaner like Shaklee's Basic H or Amway's L.O.C. when in the mountains. They can take care to leave human wastes a good distance away from water supplies. Also, leave as much of your soap suds as possible away from the water supply.*

As mentioned previously, *never cut switchbacks.* Trails can be greatly damaged by cutting switchbacks; so please do not do it.

Finally, use only deadwood lying on the ground for a fire. Never cut wood off of live trees. If you expect to go into an area that may be lacking in wood, take a stove, not a hatchet.

Lest this chapter sound negativistic, it must be said that it is. In the last few years I have revisited many places that I had visited on my first backpacking trips. In every case each area had suffered some damage over the years from careless backpackers. *This tide of degradation can be stopped only if backpackers acquire a sense of responsibility for their wilderness areas. The backpacker who drops but one gum wrapper on the ground has no right to accuse the other backpacker of leaving a messy campsite, for in his act of dropping that gum wrapper, he has provided a bad example for those who follow. In this simple act of carelessness, he has given a rationale for an inexcusably bad habit to the novice backpacker who follows.* In his act, he gives the novice an excuse to say, "I saw litter along the trail; it will not make any difference if I leave just this one little can here."

Only by setting an example for others and letting them know what is expected of them can we keep our wilderness areas beautiful and free of civilization's pollutants. Leave trails and campsites as clean as or cleaner than you found them. Many wilderness lovers carry out the trash of less considerate campers. In doing so they help make the woods more beautiful to those who will follow and they derive the satisfaction of helping keep America beautiful. Such persons deserve great praise!

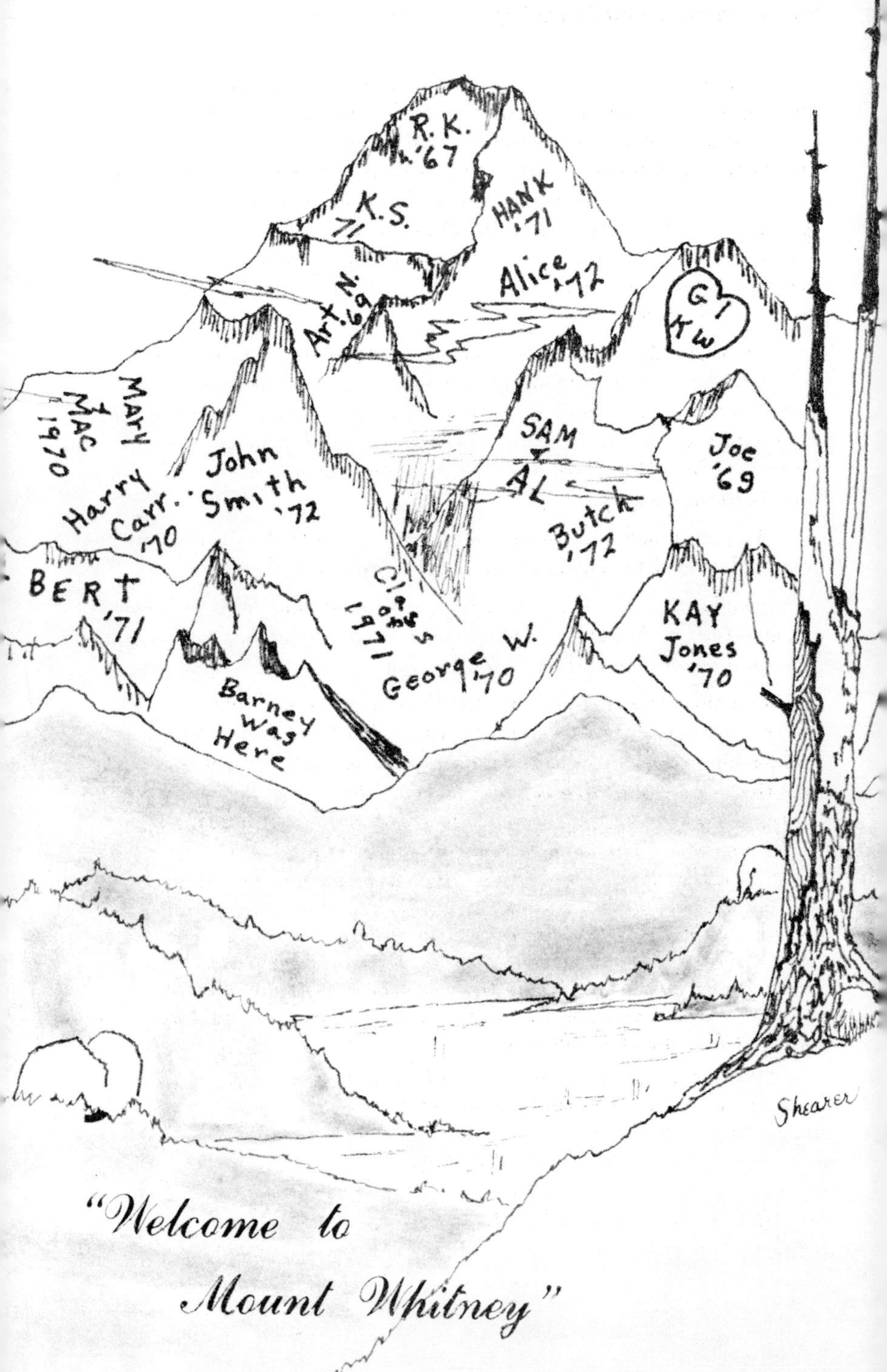

R.K. '67
K.S. '71
HANK '71
Alice '72
Art N. '69
G♡KW
Mary Mac 1970
SAM
Joe '69
Harry Carr '70
John Smith '72
AL
Butch '72
BERT '71
Class of '71
KAY Jones '70
Barney Was Here
George W. '70

Shearer

"Welcome to
Mount Whitney"

CHAPTER 12

LET'S GO AND WHERE TO GO

The preceding chapters have tried to provide you with the techniques that make for a successful backpacking trip. Despite this advice, purchasing the best equipment and using the most sophisticated mountain techniques will not automatically ensure a pleasurable backpacking experience. Deciding upon where to go deserves just as much consideration as deciding which sleeping bag to purchase.

All too often people take off on a backpacking trip with very little knowledge of where they are going. The results can be unfortunate.

Often a trip is ruined by bad weather, mosquitoes, impassable passes or a thousand and one other ills. Naturally, the sun will not shine every day, and other impediments will arise to dim your enjoyment of the wilderness. Nevertheless, a little predeparture planning can pay off handsomely.

Now, I am not so naive as to assume that readers of this book purchased it merely to find out what backpacking is all about. Most readers have already decided to go backpacking and probably know exactly where they are going.

Why not stop just a minute and ask yourself: What made me decide to go backpacking there? Perhaps you were stirred by a friend telling of his exploits. Perhaps you were intrigued by the thought of hiking over some of the highest passes in the country. Possibly you were emboldened by the tales of daring brought back by an acquaintance. A more likely explanation is that you desire to repeat the journey made by one of your friends. You are, in short, a copycat.

Now there is nothing wrong with being a copycat. I have been following trails forged by my fellow backpackers for years. One must bear in mind, however, that what held true for your friend last year will not necessarily hold true for you this year. It is absolutely impossible to know with certainty that travel over one given trail that was a delight last year will be similarly enjoyable this year.

That marvelous hiking trail that Uncle John took last July might be covered with snow this July. Possibly, that beautiful canyon that so-and-so's friend hiked up last June will be deluged with rain this June. And it is not altogether unlikely that you will not even be permitted to hike into the same area this year because of a high risk of forest fire.

The point being made here is: do not put all your eggs in one basket. Do not *commit* yourself to retracing the steps made by someone else a year before. If you do, you may be disappointed.

Leave yourself open. Choose one or two good wilderness areas, then map out *several* prospective hikes. Start doing this well in advance of your departure date.

If you do not know what the area is like, consult trail guides (available in most mountain shops) and friends. A letter to the United States Forest Service or to the National Park Service might help. Finally, try to delay a final decision on your exact route until you have completely evaluated these factors:

(1) Your physical condition
(2) Terrain
(3) Weather
(4) Transportation problems

(1) *Foremost consideration should be given to your physical condition.* As the old expression goes, do not bite off more than you can chew. Try yourself out. Take a short (five to fifteen miles) weekend backpacking trip into familiar country.

Preparation of your body is as important as preparation of your equipment. A couple of hard weekends "in training" can pay off handsomely when the trail starts up the side of the mountain. You will feel better and perform better if you are in good shape.

Unfortunately, there is no shortcut to good physical condition. Most people over twenty will find it necessary to start a daily regimen of exercise at least one month before departing on a major backpacking trip. Do not be afraid to exercise. There is nothing wrong with getting a few sore muscles, but do not *strain* your muscles. Work yourself into an exercise program gradually.

A thirty-year-old office worker is only asking for trouble if he tries to run an eight-minute mile with no preconditioning. Ease yourself into an exercise program gradually. If you condition yourself properly, you will not be sorry.

In all my years of hiking, I have never met one person who said he was sorry about taking the time to condition himself. Furthermore, proper conditioning can put an older person in better physical shape than a person half his age.

I have seen scores of forty- and fifty-year-old Boy Scout leaders hiking along the trail with their proteges, in as good if not better condition than their students.

(2) *What is the terrain like?* What we are referring to here are the ups and downs of the trail.

As the saying goes: "There are forty-mile hikes, and there are forty-mile hikes." I am familiar with forty-mile stretches of wilderness trail that can be covered in two days without too much trouble. I am also familiar with forty-mile stretches of trail which I would allocate at least five days to traverse. Why the great disparity? Is a mile not a mile? No.

On a well-graded flat or slightly downhill stretch, a good hiker can travel 2½-3 miles in one hour. On a slight uphill stretch a good hiker can travel about 2 miles per hour. On a very hard uphill trail at high altitude, a hiker is lucky to go 1 mile in an hour.

Keep this in mind in planning out your hike. Obtain topographical maps and examine the uphill and downhill stretches of a trail that will be encountered along the way. Try to find out firsthand what it means to hike up 1000 vertical feet. In time you will realize that in the mountains the number of miles that you have traveled does not mean quite as much as the vertical ascents and descents that you have encountered.

Experienced backpackers plan out their trip with an eye to the topographic characteristics of the terrain as well as the miles they will cover.

Novices should be especially wary of trails which alternate between ascents of steep passes and quick descents into river canyons. Careful reading of topographic maps will generally reveal the presence of such geographic features.

Finally, there is no substitute for firsthand knowledge. A friend who has traveled over the same trail before is your best source of advice. Also, you should always consult the local park rangers before setting out.

(3) *What is the weather going to be like?* This is not as absurd a question as it sounds. Naturally, it is not possible to predict the exact weather conditions in a given area weeks or even days in advance. Nevertheless, with a little good planning and luck, one can do a great deal to promote the enjoyment of a backpacking trip.

Three weather factors must be taken into consideration: snow on the ground, air temperature, and possibility of rainshowers.

If there is too much snow on the ground, it will be difficult if not impossible to cross over any mountain pass. For instance, 1971 was an especially bad year for backpacking in the northwest. Because of snow, most of the high mountain passes stayed closed until August. Some trails were never even opened, officially. One can best avoid snowbound passes by planning a trip for August; however, in years of lighter snowfall one can easily cross the highest passes in June.

Next, check out the temperature conditions so that you will have the right clothes along. If the nights are especially cold, do not hesitate to bring along a suit of long underwear to keep you snug.

Finally, check out the possibility of rain. As a rule, weather fronts are uncommon in the western mountains during the summer months. Rainfall is usually the result of local thunder showers. Occasionally, however, a rainfront will move through (this is most common in western Washington and Oregon). If you are a fair-weather hiker like myself, you will maintain extra plans and maps for a hike in a different area. I made good use of those extra plans in August of 1971. Weeks in advance I had planned a trip into the North Cascades of Washington state. When I arrived there, a weather front was starting to move through, and there was no prospect for clearing over the next three days. Having prepared for this eventuality, I packed up my gear and headed south. A one-day drive took me to a beautiful United States Forest Service Campground near Bend, Oregon. The next morning I started out on a five-day hike in the Three Sisters' Wilderness area, during which I encountered nothing but bright sunny days.

Naturally, everyone will not encounter such marvelous luck, but such an experience points up the value of contingency planning. Do not lock yourself up by irrevocably committing yourself to one hike. Give yourself several alternative routes so that if the weather turns sour, you will not be left "holding the bag."

As departure day approaches, stay abreast of the latest weather conditions and forecasts. Also, do not hesitate to call up the park or forest ranger in the area you intend to visit. Ask him for his latest weather reports. Find out how the snow levels are in the passes.

These people live in the area and work on the trails you will be traveling over. They are familiar with weather patterns and the snow levels. Telephone the ranger station nearest to your proposed trailhead and ask about the weather and trail conditions. They will give you better answers than the weatherman on local radio or television.

(4) *How are you getting there?* Most of us live in cities and travel by either bus or automobile. Rural areas seldom offer the public transportation facilities of a city; thus one most probable form of transportation to the trailhead will be the automobile.

If your trailhead is in mountainous country—as it probably will be—be sure the car is running well. Special attention should be given to brakes and cooling systems. When going up steep grades or over high passes, shift to low gear and turn off air conditioning devices. When you leave your car, check to be sure that all lights are out and that the handbrake is set. Finally, to avoid tempting burglars, store *everything* that you will not take with you either under the seats or in the trunk.

While an automobile can get you to your trailhead quickly, it can also present you with a few problems. Paramount among these is what I call the "return liability factor." This is the matter of returning to your car at the end of your hike. There are several ways of accomplishing this:

1. Accept the undesirable alternative of backtracking to the trailhead over the same trail.

2. Plan a circular trip which takes you away from and back to your car on a trail which does not backtrack on itself. This is called a loop trip. With a few maps and a little time one should have little trouble finding a trail loop that will return you to a point at or near your automobile.

3. Arrange a ferrying system with some companions in your party so that you pick them up at the terminus trailhead (at the start of the trip) and they return you to the starting trailhead (at the end of the trip).

4. Trade cars with some friends who are hiking the same trail in the opposite direction. (Do not forget to get the keys.)

5. Hitchhike back to your car. It is quite easy to hitch with a backpack. In most mountain areas in the west, the local populace is aware of the lack of transportation and therefore willing to help backpackers out.

More often than not, backpackers—especially older ones—choose one of the first two methods of getting around the "return liability factor." It is easier and creates less anxiety in their minds. Nevertheless, it restricts their outdoor experience greatly.

By choosing one of the first two methods, a person limits his outdoor experience to the distance he can hike away from his automobile. It also deprives a person of the experience of ever traversing an entire mountain range. Only a backpacker who has done so can describe the great satisfaction of accomplishing this feat. Many persons can say they drove over the Rockies or Sierra. You could say that you walked over them.

Some persons might be in a position where it is either impossible or undesirable to take their own car to the trailhead. This should in no way deter you from going backpacking. Why not travel to your trailhead by bus? Travel by bus in the west is both comfortable and cheap. While bus service to trailheads may not be the best possible, it can usually be accomplished by hitchhiking or hiring a taxi in the nearest town.

Taking a bus can often be more economical for two persons than driving your own car. You eliminate the "return liability factor," and you eliminate the possibility of having your car damaged.

Bus transportation generally costs three cents to five cents per mile and few automobiles can be operated for less than that. Thus even a cost benefit can be derived by "leaving the driving to them."

Should you find bus travel unacceptable, consider flying. While flying is costly, it is quick. When combined with other means of transportation, an airplane can wisk you off to almost anywhere in one day's time. Moreover, many persons with limited vacation time choose this as their prime source of transportation to the trailhead. During the past two years I have personally encountered three backpacking parties who flew out to the western mountains from the east coast solely to go backpacking.

Even if you do not have an automobile, it is still easy to travel with a backpack. Both my friends and I have done so many times, and except for a few stares, our journeys were uneventful.

The only advice for the free-traveling backpacker is: (1) pack everything in your backpack before leaving home; (2) take a bag of food to munch on during the prewilderness part of the trip; (3) put a cover over your pack when it is sent by air or in the luggage bay of a bus. This cover can be made from an old pair of blue jeans or two old towels sewn together, and will protect your pack from dirt and abrasion.

A note on hitchhiking: while most rural people are very receptive to backpackers—even long-haired ones—it is not uncommon for long-hairs to be hassled. It is always best to hitch in pairs and avoid comments which are derogatory of the people or country in which you are traveling.

In 1970 the National Park Service adopted an antihitchhiking law. The law was mainly used to prevent long-hairs from congregating in the parks, but was also used against backpackers in the summer of 1970. Since then the law has not been enforced against backpackers, but it could be. Colorado does strictly enforce its antihitchhiking law.

Where To Go

A compendium of backpacking areas would require a volume in itself. A good source of general information is the National Park Service's booklet *Back Country Travel*. It may be obtained free of charge by writing to the National Park Service, Department of Interior, Washington, DC 20240.

I have chosen a few of the backpacking areas that I know to be excellent. All of these areas have convenient roadheads and are extremely habitable during the summer season. They all have abundant water, and temperatures are moderate.

ROCKY MOUNTAIN NATIONAL PARK — This park is only a short hop from Denver and Boulder, Colorado. It offers a splendid variety of topography, ranging from spacious river canyons to soaring mountain peaks. As this part of the Rocky Mountains is relatively young geologically, mountain peaks are steep and canyons deep. This park offers some of the most spectacular scenery in the United States.

I would strongly recommend the park to novice backpackers, as there are many short "loop" trips that can be made. The advantage here is that you can easily return to where you started without having to look at the same trail twice.

Disadvantages of this park include frequent afternoon showers of a localized nature, and high altitudes (8,000 feet +). Also, this park, because of its proximity to the big cities of the midwest, is visited by a tremendous number of backpackers. As a result of this overwhelming demand on the back country the Park has moved to a *strict* reservation system. Backpackers must register before their trip, and are *assigned* a campsite for every night of the trip. For more information write Superintendent, Rocky Mountain National Park, Estes Park, CO 80517.

SIERRA NEVADA, CALIFORNIA — It is impossible to compare the Sierra Nevada with any other wilderness backpacking area in the United States. It stands in a class by itself. No other wilderness area or park offers the variety of scenery and expanse of this incredible range. One hundred years of effort by thousands of persons and notably the Sierra Club has preserved part of this vast range as one of the largest contiguous wilderness backpacking areas in the West. This indeed is a major accomplishment when one considers its proximity to California's large population centers.

This backpacking area includes Yosemite, Sequoia and King's Canyon National Parks, and major portions of the Inyo, Sierra, Sequoia and Toiyabe National Forests. It is without question the most accessible wilderness area in the West. Approaches can be made from scores of points along the eastern and western slopes of the range. The area itself contains over three thousand miles of trails maintained solely for backpacking and other nonmotorized travel.

Elevations range from 3,000 feet to over 14,000 feet, but the most enjoyable hiking is done between 7,000 and 13,000 feet, where temperatures range between 60°F. and 80°F. on most summer days. Rain is not uncommon but is most likely to come only in the late afternoon. Still, it is possible to camp out in the Sierra for over a week and never feel a drop of rain.

Terrain can be rough or relatively easy. Hikes on the lower and warmer western slopes of the range are easier than the precipitous ups and downs of the higher eastern crests. Still, the excellent quality of the trails should in no circumstances rule out an eastern crest traverse.

The biggest problem of the Sierra backpacker is deciding on a trail to take. One can come back to these mountains every year for a decade and cover only a small fraction of the trails.

Whether you want to take a short trip or stay out on the trail for a month, the Sierra offers you an unforgettable experience.

NORTH CASCADES (Washington State) — This soaring mountain range contains some of the most rugged scenery in the lower forty-eight. Lush meadows merge with snow-capped peaks. The North Cascades contain hundreds of active glaciers, remnants of the last glacial age.

Many fine short hikes can be taken in the Stevens Pass and Snoqualmie Pass areas, which are less than two hours from Seattle for even the slowest driver.

For the more hardy backpackers planning a longer trip, the North Cascades National Park and Glacier Park Wilderness area offer a mountain experience never to be forgotten. Backpacking here is strenuous, but this is compensated for by the scenery, which is unparalleled.

MOUNT RAINIER NATIONAL PARK — Within the boundaries of this fine backpacking area are 300 miles of trails. Part of the trail system completely skirts the lower slopes of the glacier-covered 14,410 foot peak.

Daytime temperatures in the North Cascades can range from warm to cool during the summer months. Rain can be frequent and an annoyance, and one should be prepared for it. Late July and August are the best months to backpack this area. In these months most of the previous winter's snow has melted, the alpine flowers are out, and the rains are somewhat less frequent.

SOUTHERN CASCADES (Oregon) — This range of mountains is primarily volcanic in origin and is somewhat less rugged than the northern part of the range. Long trips are somewhat discouraged because of the intrusion of logging into the subalpine forests, but quality makes up for quantity. Winter snows disappear in this region earlier than in the northern part of the range, and summer weather tends to be warmer.

The best backpacking country in Oregon is found in the fabulous Three Sisters' Wilderness Area west of Bend (750,000 acres). Less rugged than the mountains to the north, this area lacks none of the beauty. Snow-capped extinct volcanos form the backdrop for alpine meadows and lava flows.

YELLOWSTONE NATIONAL PARK and
GRAND TETON NATIONAL PARK (Wyoming) — These two parks constitute one of the greatest recreational areas in the nation. This wilderness area of 2,500,000 acres has every kind of scenery imaginable,

from geysers to waterfalls and from meadows to snow-capped peaks. The area possesses a variety of animal life seen in few places in America, including beaver, moose, elk, and the bald eagle.

Backpacking trips can be as long or short as you desire, as there is a tremendous trail network. The park's rangers are always willing to advise you in planning any outing.

Weather is pleasant and rain is not overly bothersome.

There are, of course, scores of other National Parks and United States Forest Service wilderness areas which are suitable for backpacking. Those areas listed above are the most popular and most frequently visited areas. Some persons may find this fact annoying in that they do not want to go to the wilderness to look at other people, but I believe that most backpackers like to meet a few other people out on the trail. There is a sort of comradery among backpackers who meet on the trail, and most persons enjoy a trail encounter. When meeting persons coming from the opposite direction, you can exchange information about the trail conditions and gain other information and advice that can be helpful. Then, of course, there is the plain enjoyment of talking to different people.

For those who prefer a more solitary wilderness outing, despair not; there are several millions of acres of mountainous wilderness areas awaiting you in the great northwestern states of Idaho, Wyoming and Montana. These three states alone contain over seven million acres of National Forest Wilderness areas, a combined area equal to three Yellowstone National Parks. These areas are seldom visited and abound in fish, fowl and animal life. Here, one can find lakes which are visited only once in a decade, trout which grow to thirty pounds, and mountains which have been climbed but once if at all.

Excellent backpacking areas in this region include the Wind River Range of Wyoming within Bridger Shoshone National Forest, the Big Horn Mountains of Wyoming within the Bighorn National Forest (Cloud Peak Primitive Area), the Sawtooth Salmon River Mountains of Idaho, the Bitterroot Mountain Range on the border of Idaho and Montana within the Selway Bitterroot Primitive Area, and the giant Lewis and Clark Range of northern Montana that encompasses Glacier National Park, Flathead National Forest and the Lewis and Clark National Forest (Bob Marshall Wilderness Area).

If these areas are still not wild enough for you, there are always roadless and unexplored Alaska and Western Canada awaiting you.

The opportunities for summer backpacking in western North America are almost unlimited. We are fortunate that such vast areas of the North American continent remain available for wilderness recreation. We owe a tremendous debt of gratitude to our forefathers, who were prudent enough to set aside portions of the American landscape for posterity. The value of the wilderness lands that are presently protected by law cannot be given a price tag. It is a birthright that must be assiduously protected and passed on to our offspring intact. In a similar sense, we must not fail to expand these lands when the opportunity presents itself.

A hundred years ago nobody could have predicted the millions of visitors to Yosemite National Park. Yet over the objections of ranching and lumbering interests, a park was established. We today must continue to guard against the misuse of recreational areas. While economics must play a part in determining resource management, it must never be the sole criterion. Recreational potential must be given equal consideration in determining resource use. One cannot put a price on a Yellowstone National Park or a redwood grove. The monetary values placed on such real estate derive strictly from the land's potential for economic exploitation. Economic values can never calculate the emotional enjoyment derived from wilderness lands. We must never lose sight of this if we are going to preserve our wilderness areas. Backpackers owe it both to themselves and to their unborn offspring to protect our wilderness lands.

More than any other group, backpackers are the trustees for America's wilderness lands. As such it is incumbent upon us to fight for the preservation and protection of this great heritage.

CHECK LIST

Use this list to check off the items necessary for each backpacking trip. Add to or subtract from the list according to your needs and the weather conditions.

- ☐ knapsack or pack frame
- ☐ sleeping bag
- ☐ tent
- ☐ plastic ground cloth

- ☐ hat or cap
- ☐ jacket
- ☐ shirt
- ☐ underwear
- ☐ socks
- ☐ trousers
- ☐ shorts
- ☐ swim suit
- ☐ tennis shoes
- ☐ boots
- ☐ hankerchief
- ☐ poncho
- ☐ gloves
- ☐ dark glasses

- ☐ cup
- ☐ spoon
- ☐ salt
- ☐ soda
- ☐ sugar
- ☐ cook stove
- ☐ can for cooking
- ☐ powdered coffee, tea, bouillon dried fruits, nuts and seeds

- toilet paper ☐
- lip balm ☐
- insect repellent ☐
- comb ☐
- water purifying tablets ☐
- sunburn salve ☐
- snake bite kit ☐
- ace bandage ☐
- iodine ☐
- bandaids ☐
- sewing kit ☐
- extra shoe laces ☐
- soap ☐
- nylon cord ☐
- books: plant identification ☐
- birds ☐
- mammal tracks ☐
- notebook and pencil ☐
- waterproof bags for * ☐
- *maps ☐
- *camera, film ☐
- *fishing license ☐
- *matches ☐
- compass ☐
- canteen ☐
- watch ☐
- pocket knife ☐
- flashlight ☐

REFERENCES

American Red Cross, *First Aid Textbook,* Doubleday & Co., Garden City, N.Y., 1957.

Angier, Bradford, *How to Stay Alive in the Woods,* Collier Books, New York, 1962.

Bates, Marston, *The Natural History of Mosquitoes,* Macmillan Co., New York, 1949.

Boyd, Bud, *Bud Boyd's Guide to Hunting and Fishing in California,* Chronicle Publishing Co., San Francisco, 1960.

Cardwell, Paul, Jr., *America's Camping Book,* Charles Scribner's Sons, New York, 1969.

Dyar, *Mosquitoes of the Americas,* Carnegie Institute Publications, New York, 1928.

Farquahar, Francis P., *History of the Sierra Nevada,* University of California Press, Berkeley & Los Angeles, 1969.

Hardin, Garrett, *Biology: Its Principles and Implications,* W.H. Freeman & Co., San Francisco & London, 1966.

Holden, John L., *Camping,* Cornerstone Library Publications, New York, 1969.

Holum, John R., *Elements of General & Biological Chemistry,* John Wiley & Sons, New York, 1962.

Johnson, James Ralph, *Anyone Can Backpack in Comfort,* David McKay Co., New York, 1965.

Kirk, Donald, *Wild Edible Plants of the Western United States,* Naturegraph Publishers, Healdsburg, California, 1971.

Leechman, Douglas, *The Hiker's Handbook,* W.W. Norton & Co., New York, 1944.

Leopold, Aldo, *A Sand County Almanac,* Oxford University Press, New York, 1968.

Marshall, Spring & Mueller, *100 Hikes in Western Washington,* The Mountaineers, Seattle, 1966 (Printer: Craftsman Press.)

McCracken, Harold, *The Beast That Walks Like Man,* Hanover House, Garden City, N.Y., 1955.

Muir, John, *My First Summer in the Sierra,* Repr. of 1911 Ed., Greenwood, Boston & New York.

Muir, John, *The Mountains of California,* American Museum of Natural History, Garden City, N.Y., 1961.

Ovington, Ray, *Tactics on Trout*, Alfred A. Knopf, New York, 1969.

Rathmel, R. C., *Backpacking*, R. C. Rathmel, 1968 (Printer: The Alamogordo Printing Co., Alamorgordo, N.M.).

Sierra Club, *Sierra Club Bulletin*, Sierra Club, San Francisco, assorted issues 1961-1971.

Slaymaker, S.R. II, *Simplified Fly Fishing*, Harper and Row, New York, 1969.

Stevens, Montague, *Meet Mr. Grizzly*, The University of New Mexico Press, Albuquerque, 1943.

Sweet, Muriel, *Common Edible and Useful Plants of the West*, Naturegraph Publishers, Healdsburg, California, 1962.

Wright, William H., *The Black Bear*, Charles Scribner's Sons, New York, 1910.

THE AMERICAN WILDLIFE REGION SERIES, a series of books on the wildlife and plants of specific wilderness areas, with hundreds of illustrations. Send to Naturegraph Publishers, Healdsburg, Cal. 95448 for a free catalog.